"T. J. Addington gives us a timely challenge to reevaluate our lives in the context of God's purposes and to 'Live as if we mean it.' His great talent is to communicate in such a way that the passion for the underlying message is illuminated, but never obscured by the elegance of the prose. This is the testament of a man who is clearly 'living' as though he means it."

—LORD BATES OF LANGBAURGH, deputy chairman of the Conservative Party, founder of Walton Bates (Management Consultants), and formerly Her Majesty's Paymaster General

"The best way to live life is with inspired intentionality. T. J. Addington helps us to do just that! In *Live Like You Mean It*, he faithfully offers a steady compass for such a well-lived life. Don't just read it—live it!"

—REVEREND EDMUND CHAN, senior pastor, Covenant Evangelical Free Church

"This book offers experienced leaders (whether in the church or in the secular world) an organized set of questions to guide one through the tough and challenging decisions one needs to make. It contains leadership keys for both U.S.-based leaders and those leading in an international setting."

—RON TSCHETTER, former director, United States Peace Corps

"I highly recommend this book to anyone searching for ways to become more effective for the kingdom. There is a call of God to reevaluate our lives and ministries, taking an honest look at how to find a deeper satisfaction and greater kingdom impact. Addington guides us through self-discovery by asking ten vital, life-changing questions that will enable each believer to leave a legacy of fruitful ministry."

—JACKIE REDMOND, director of EFCA RESOUND Women's Ministry

"T. J. Addington takes readers on an ever-deepening journey to figure out how God has uniquely created us and the good works He's eagerly waiting for us to engage in. The multitude of questions Addington provides are pivotal, especially when explored with close friends. If we honestly answer them, we'll escape the busyness roller coaster and instead climb aboard a lifetime ride of amazing significance."

—DIANE J. MCDOUGALL, editorial director, Journey Group; editor, *EFCA Today* magazine

"Want to get real help in living a meaningful life? T. J. Addington asks the important questions that will help you along. He knows and lives of that which he writes."

—GRANT E. NELSON, retired CFO, West Publishing Company

"In *Live Like You Mean It*, T. J. Addington shares engaging real-life examples of how people who set goals for their lives and focus their time on these priorities experience fulfilling results. He also asks thought-provoking questions for personal application and provides group discussion questions. This book is perfectly designed to help us realize the power of personal life planning. It helps us identify our own priorities and share our thoughts with others, thus enhancing our commitment to living like we mean it. Addington has provided a great guide that will help readers live the full life for which God has wired them."

—CATHIE LEIMBACH, cofounder and consulting partner, STRIVE!

"T. J. Addington has done it again! In *Live Like You Mean It*, he addresses real-life key questions and issues that most of us struggle with. He gives us sound biblically based solutions and answers that can help us start realizing the potential that God has given each of us."

—KEN LARSON, CEO and founder, Slumberland Furniture

"If you are looking for a succinct and personal guide to finding and living a significant 'no regrets' life, this book is it!"

—ELIZABETH MARING, JD, general counsel, ADW Group, LLC

"T. J. Addington masterfully practices the art of asking great questions. *Live Like You Mean It* is one of the most coherent and compelling sets of questions for effective living that I have read."

—DR. BRUCE MCNICOL, author, *Bo's Café, TrueFaced, The Ascent*

T. J. ADDINGTON

LIVE
LIKE YOU
MEAN IT

The 10 Crucial Questions That Will Help You

- Clarify Your Purpose

- Live Intentionally

- Make the Most of the Rest of Your Life

NAVPRESS ⦿

NAVPRESS⬤

NavPress is the publishing ministry of The Navigators, an international Christian organization and leader in personal spiritual development. NavPress is committed to helping people grow spiritually and enjoy lives of meaning and hope through personal and group resources that are biblically rooted, culturally relevant, and highly practical.

For a free catalog go to www.NavPress.com
or call 1.800.366.7788 in the United States or 1.800.839.4769 in Canada.

© 2010 by T. J. Addington

ISBN: 978-1-60006-673-3

Cover design by Arvid Wallen

Some of the anecdotal illustrations in this book are true to life and are included with the permission of the persons involved. All other illustrations are composites of real situations, and any resemblance to people living or dead is coincidental.

Unless otherwise identified, all Scripture quotations in this publication are taken from the *Holy Bible, New International Version*° (NIV°). Copyright © 1973, 1978, 1984 by International Bible Society. Used by permission of Zondervan. All rights reserved. Other versions used include: *THE MESSAGE* (MSG). Copyright © 1993, 1994, 1995, 1996, 2000, 2001, 2002. Used by permission of NavPress Publishing Group; and the *Holy Bible*, New Living Translation (NLT), copyright © 1996, 2004. Used by permission of Tyndale House Publishers, Inc., Wheaton, Illinois 60189. All rights reserved.

Library of Congress Cataloging-in-Publication Data
Addington, T. J.
  Live like you mean it : the 10 crucial questions that will help you clarify your purpose, live intentionally, make the most of the rest of your life / T.J. Addington.
    p. cm.
  Includes bibliographical references.
  ISBN 978-1-60006-673-3
  1. Christian life. I. Title.
  BV4501.3.A345 2010
  248.4--dc22
                                    2009026156

Printed in the United States of America

2 3 4 5 6 7 8 / 14 13 12 11 10

This book is dedicated with love and appreciation to Doug Rhoda, a friend and hero who reached the finish line in February 2008 with faith and perseverance. And to Susan Rhoda, a woman of deep faith and dignity, and a friend for life.

CONTENTS

FOREWORD

We give too many answers and ask too few questions.

Jesus understood what children instinctively know and most adults have forgotten: It is in wrestling with questions, and not giving answers, that we grow and change. That is why in Jesus' interactions with people He asked a staggering number of questions. For a question is full of possibility. A question demands that you give attention, that your mind should open up. Questions can change the world. The right questions will change your life.

That is why I am so excited about this book.

We ask far too few questions about life, and when we do, we often ask the wrong questions. The most important questions are not about us at all, but about a deeper reality that calls to us beyond the smallness of our lives. The right questions — and above all, the great questions about God — open the door to meaning and hope.

This book asks the right questions — questions that go to the core of God's call on our lives and our willingness to live at the intersection of His call and our response. Right questions can lead to right answers, but if you never ask the question, you will never know the answer.

Take a moment and look at the table of content for the ten questions T. J. tackles in this book. Every human being needs to ask them, and how we answer will deeply affect the quality of our lives and the legacy that we leave. Thoughtful people mull on these kinds of questions, but T. J. has done us a huge service by clarifying the most important ones and framing them in a simple way. I cannot imagine anyone I know or care for who does not need to reflect and respond.

In a day when many Christ followers are desiring to follow more closely and live more strategically, T. J. provides us with a biblical foundation for how we approach life. It is a *God*-centered life rather than a *me*-centered life, where His priorities are central to everything we do. It is a life of balance rather than frenetic activity where we have the time to think deeply and focus on the priorities God has given us. It is a life where we create space for God to grow us—so that our hearts become more like His heart.

God formed each of us in a unique way and designed us for a unique kingdom work. Too often we have been given cookie-cutter approaches to how we live out that call or relate to God. This is not a book about formulas but about reality. As you thoughtfully work your way through *Live Like You Mean It*, you will gain insight into *your* wiring, *your* unique relationship with God, and the contribution that *you* can make in *your* circles of influence—whether a boardroom or a neighborhood. You will also learn simple ways to live intentionally rather than accidentally and how to connect God's priorities for your life with your actual schedule.

You will be challenged not only by the questions T. J. asks but by the accounts of real people living out their faith in unique but meaningful ways. They are people who have said yes to God and have made Him the center of their lives, even when times are tough. They are ordinary people leaving an eternal legacy in simple but profound ways. If all of us caught that vision for our lives, our communities would be transformed by the love of Jesus and the small bits of heaven that His people bring to a broken world.

My hope is that you will live like you mean it! For the sake of Jesus, the influence you have, and the legacy you will leave.

And for the joy.

—JOHN ORTBERG
pastor, Menlo Park Presbyterian Church, Menlo Park, California;
author, *If You Want to Walk on Water, You've Got to Get Out of the Boat*,
The Life You've Always Wanted, and *Faith & Doubt*

ACKNOWLEDGMENTS

It is with appreciation that I thank my prayer partner of twenty years, Naomi Fausch, who at age one hundred has faithfully prayed for me over many years.

I owe great thanks to the staff of United Hospital, St. Paul, who provided extraordinary care from December 4, 2007, to January 14, 2008, and to those who contributed to my rehabilitation. Without their care, this book would not have been written. I thank my faithful prayer team, parents, friends, and extended family, who stood with my family in our long hour of need, and my sons, Jon and Steven, who supported Mary Ann with maturity beyond their age. And finally, to Mary Ann, whose courage, love, faith, and tenacity through my illness and recovery will forever be remembered as a supreme gift.

Thanks to Shawn and Sally Weimer, who remain faithful despite the sorrow of the loss of their dear son, Zach—an example and inspiration to us all. Their willingness to share their story in this book will be an encouragement to many.

I thank each one mentioned in this book. You are examples of people living out God's call on your lives, and each of you has influenced my own journey.

To Mike Miller and the team at NavPress, I express thanks for their encouragement with this project, and to Keith Wall for his editing expertise. And lastly, to Grant and Carol for providing a wonderful haven for writing in Big Sky, Montana.

INTRODUCTION

All of us have dreams for our lives. They may involve family, work, success, influence, or fulfilling some deep passion. Ultimately, though, our dreams are about living a life of significance. We want to know that our lives count. We want to accomplish something of meaning during our years on earth.

Yet we are often disappointed that our dreams are not fulfilled and that we don't accomplish what we wish we had. This book is designed to help you get where you want to go — to live life like you mean it! And in the process it will help to remove the barriers that keep you from becoming everything God designed you to be and accomplishing everything He has for you.

If answering ten key questions had the potential to change your life for the better, would you take the time to find the answers? That is the proposition I am presenting to you in this book.

Life is full of questions that demand answers. The problem is knowing which questions are critical and which are ancillary. I believe that the ten questions posed in this book are the most essential questions you could ever ponder. They have the potential to be "game changers" because they will help you think deeply about the most important issues of your life, clarify your purpose, maximize your strengths, and fulfill your God-given potential.

Think of your life as a huge puzzle with thousands of pieces. Those pieces make up who you are, what you think, how you choose to live, how you make decisions, how you see yourself, and the myriad bits that comprise your life. Imagine that the pieces are spread out on a table in front of you and the challenge is to make sense of the whole — but to do that you have to put the puzzle together.

The puzzle's instructions say that if you can find ten key pieces, the rest of the puzzle will start to fall into place quickly. But *you* have to figure out which are the ten key pieces that will allow you to put the rest together in order to see the complete picture.

This book contains those ten key pieces. If you put those pieces together, the rest of life will start to make much more sense and you'll be better able to achieve your God-given dreams.

These ten questions are ones that every person should wrestle with because they influence everything we are and do. I want to encourage you — whatever your stage of life — to deal with the questions now so that your years ahead will be as fulfilling and fruitful as possible. The fact that you have even picked up this book means you are intrigued by the proposition and want to make the most of your life.

Our guide through this journey is Scripture. You can ask ultimate questions only if there is the possibility of ultimate answers, and I believe that the ultimate answers are found in the Bible. Whether or not you claim to be a Christ follower, God's Word can help you understand the narrative of your life. And if He becomes a part of that narrative, your life will be far richer and more rewarding.

This book does not spell out all the answers for you. Instead, this is a book of self-exploration and self-discovery. It is a road map revealing how God made you and how He wants to use you. Only you can discern the answers for your life. But if you never ask the questions, you will never know the answers.

Live Like You Mean It is written for everyone who desires to understand his or her life in a new way. It is written for executives and construction workers, stay-at-home moms and career women, high schoolers or college students, entry-level employees and retirees. The more people who consider these questions and come to conclusions, the greater our world will be for it. This book is not written for an elite few but for all of us who care about living a life of intentionality and meaning.

And if you feel like you're stuck in a rut or lacking direction, this book is especially for you. Life has a way of getting overly familiar, and familiarity starts to destroy our spirit of adventure, zeal, and enthusiasm. I want to help you reignite the passion and purpose for life that God designed you to have.

This is not a difficult book to read or apply. But it will challenge you to ask and answer key questions that, if applied, will affect your life in significant ways. Each question is worth your careful consideration before moving on; take the time to answer the questions. Unlike many books that are simply inspirational, this one is practical. It will help you accomplish what you want to achieve with your life. Your participation by making notes and answering specific questions will help you get the most out of the experience.

One more thing before we move forward: If possible, read this book with a friend or a group so that you can share your discoveries and test them with others who know you well. Important questions invite discussion, which is exactly what this book does. When you read it with others and share your insights, you will glean so much more from the process.

If you want to clarify your purpose, live smarter, and make the most of the rest of your life, take seriously the challenge presented in the pages ahead. Ponder deeply the questions raised — and be ready for God's Spirit to move you in new and exciting directions.

Chapter 1

WHY AM I HERE?

PINPOINTING YOUR PURPOSE

For we are God's workmanship, created in Christ Jesus to do good works, which God prepared in advance for us to do.

— EPHESIANS 2:10

One day when my son Jon was young, he told me that his mom was important because she was a nurse who saved people from dying. For several minutes he waxed eloquently about the significance of Mom and her work.

"What about me, Jon?" I asked when he had finished singing his mother's praises. "What do I do?"

"Oh," he said, "you're just an ordinary worker."

This is amusing, but he put his finger on how many of us probably feel about ourselves. We regard ourselves as just "ordinary people" of no special significance. Still, deep down, we desperately want our lives to count for something beyond just being here. And when we compare ourselves to others, we often think, *I wish I could have the impact they have. Or I wish I had their education or social status or wealth so my life could count just as much.*

Stop for a moment and reread the verse at the start of this chapter. In fact, I want you to personalize it: "For *I* am God's workmanship, created in Christ Jesus to do good works, which God prepared in advance for *me* to do." Did you catch what Paul said? We are God's special creation, His workmanship. If we spoke Greek like Paul did, we would know that the word *workmanship* means "a work of art" or "a one-of-a-kind creation." His masterwork! There is and has been no one like you and there never will be again.

That's not all. You were created to live in relationship with God's Son, for we were "created in Christ Jesus." This is the reason life lacks meaning when we don't live in connection and relationship with Jesus. When we enter into a personal relationship with God, His ultimate masterpiece is seen because our lives are infused with His life and our character is changed into His character. That is what gives our lives significance and purpose.

God's first masterwork is seen when we are born. Anyone who has had a child knows how amazing it is to watch each new and unique creation grow and develop. Why else do grandparents insist on showing everyone pictures of their grandkids? Because they're masterpieces! God's second masterwork takes place when we invite Christ into our lives and He transforms us. Now we see the full extent of God's masterpiece, for the first creation (birth) and the second creation (new birth) are combined into a beautiful work of unique art.

Astonishingly, God created us to join Him both in relationship and in His work in this world. "For we are God's workmanship, created in Christ Jesus *to do good works, which God prepared in advance for us to do*" (emphasis added). Not only are you and I unique, but we were uniquely designed to do something for God that only we can do. Long before the world began, long before our lives came to be, God had a plan for the gifts and wiring He would create in us and the unique ways we could contribute to His work. Therefore, if we can understand why God placed us on the earth and the unique ways that we can contribute to His work, our lives will have eternal significance.

You may be the CEO of a Fortune 500 company or the receptionist at the front desk. You may be wealthy or poor or somewhere in between. You may be highly educated or uneducated. You may be young or one hundred years old like my friend Naomi. Whoever you are and whatever your status, you were created for relationship with God and gifted for a unique role.

Joni Eareckson Tada was just seventeen years old when she spent a day with her family on the water. Diving in, she hit her head on a rock and was instantly paralyzed for life—a quadriplegic. She had everything going for her and suddenly, in an instant, life irrevocably changed. The process of rehabilitation for Joni was both physically and emotionally excruciating. She struggled with many difficult questions: What's the point of life? Why did God allow this to happen? What meaning can my life have now?

In time, Joni came to realize two amazing truths. First, she was created for relationship with Jesus. When she acknowledged this, what had been an "academic" relationship with Him started to go deeper. Today, Joni has an amazingly close relationship with God; it is clearly evident just being in her presence.

The second truth that came to Joni was that God had created her for work that was specially designed for her. She started to minister to those who had physical challenges like her and those who were marginalized by society because of physical or mental challenges. Today, through her international ministry Joni and Friends, she touches thousands of lives around our globe.

When Joni came to our church to minister, she met a young man named Michael. Fourteen years old, Michael had a degenerative condition called Batten disease. The disease had ravaged his body and mind, taken his eyesight and ability to speak, and greatly reduced his life expectancy. It has been a long, hard struggle for Michael and his family. Even with the effects of the disease on his mind, Michael met in Joni someone who could understand him. Those who watched Joni pray for Michael and saw his happy face will never forget the scene—especially afterward, when he slowly picked up her hand and kissed it.

It does not matter who you are or what your circumstances, you are a special masterpiece of God created for relationship with Him and for a specific work. That is true for Michael; it is true for Joni; and it is true for you.

DISCERNING YOUR ASSIGNMENT

I love asking people, "Why were you put on earth?" It is a question that most have not thought about. But when they start to get a glimpse of the answer, their faces light up with the understanding that they have a unique role to play in God's plan.

I'll mention my wife, Mary Ann, as an example. It is not uncommon for people to tell me, "Mary Ann is the most loving person I have ever met." She exudes grace for hurting and troubled people. She has super-sensitive radar for people who need love, encouragement, or help, and she has the ability to find solutions to problems and bring others together to see needs met. There is no judgment in her view of people; rather, her attitude is one of love, mercy, and forgiveness. Without a doubt, Mary Ann's unique role is that of extending the grace of Jesus to those who need it. God designed and wired her for this transformational assignment.

My friend Grant was a senior executive in a well-known nationwide company. He is one of the most generous people I have ever met. God has blessed him and his wife, Carol, with significant financial resources, which they use to advance God's work. Grant has an uncanny ability to think strategically, and he uses that gift to help his church and other ministries think about how to maximize their ministry influence. When I asked Grant why God placed him on this earth, he said, "To advance His kingdom." And everything he does is designed to achieve that.

Grant's wife, Carol, models the character of Christ in a wonderful way. She has the gift of hospitality and loves to help others. Carol makes all who come to their home — and they come from all walks of life and all places in their faith journey — feel comfortable and welcomed. Carol's assignment from God has everything to do with extending His love to others through her kindness and compassion.

My friends Bob and Judy share the good news of Jesus wherever they are. They were made for evangelism and for funding outreach efforts from the resources God has given them. Even on vacation in Mexico, their purpose has been applied as they have led locals to Christ. They have also been active in starting a new church. I have known Bob and Judy for years, and their passion for evangelism has been evident every time I've been with them. God has wired and gifted them for that ministry.

My son Steven is twenty-one and an avid outdoorsman. He's quite happy if you give him a knife, a bedroll, and a few basics and send him into the wilderness. He spends his summers guiding inner-city kids in the boundary waters of northern Minnesota, using the lessons of the wilderness to share spiritual lessons with these kids.

Ever since he was young, Steven has been the pied piper of the neighborhood. Kids love him and he loves them—even the kids no one else loves. When Steven was living with us, one of those marginalized kids would often come to our door. He would ask, "Can Steven come out to play?" When I would tell him that Steven was not home, he would say, "Can Maggie come out to play?" Maggie was our beagle. If Maggie was not available, he would ask if I could come out to play! But Steven was always his first choice.

Steven did not have an easy go of it in grade school. He had a reading disability that was not diagnosed until third grade. Through grade school he struggled not only to keep up but also to understand that he, too, was gifted. With his disability, he did not find academics as easy as his older brother did. But he was, and is, extraordinarily gifted in relationships. Steven's hardships gave him an understanding of the underdog and a love for those who struggle.

You may not be able to immediately answer the question, "Why did God place you on earth?" That's okay. As you work through the questions in this book, the answer to this all-important question will become clearer. And once you understand the answer, you will feel liberated to use your gifts and fulfill your destiny in God's kingdom.

As I mentally think through my friends and family members, I am amazed at the variety of answers there are to this question. People might say they were put on earth to:

- Bring others into a relationship with Jesus
- Bring Christ's values to the marketplace
- Extend the grace of Jesus to others

- Generously fund God's work
- Come alongside hurting children
- Bring significance to the marginalized
- Teach God's Word
- Help hurting people become whole
- Love the unloved
- Use the gift of hospitality to minister to others
- Provide strategic leadership to ministry ventures
- Be a voice of justice for the oppressed and poor
- Exercise the gift of faith through prayer
- Use the arts to help people think deeply about life
- Provide care for those who cannot care for themselves
- Spread the joy of being a child of God

You may consider yourself an "ordinary person," but the truth is that God has an extraordinary work for you in His kingdom that *only you* can fulfill.

IT IS *WHO*, NOT *WHAT*

God's assignment for us is not dependent on our income or social status or what kind of work we do for a living. His unique assignment is all about who He has made us to be and how He has gifted us to participate in His work. Society places a premium on income, position, and status; God places no premium on those things. Jesus is the great equalizer—He gives equal value, regard, honor, and opportunity to all people.

I vividly remember special services at a church I attended while growing up where people would share what God was doing in their lives. At each service, an elderly, poor, mentally challenged gentleman, dressed in worn secondhand clothes, would stand and tearfully thank God for all of His blessings. I'm not sure I have ever met anyone who was more grateful to God—or happier—than that man.

You know what that fellow did for a living? He pulled a wagon from house to house picking up newspapers that he would then take to recycling. In the eyes of the world, he was truly a nobody—someone to be pitied. But in God's eyes, he was as significant as anyone else in that church or community. If I had to guess why God placed him on the earth, I'd say it was to share the joy of knowing Jesus and to praise his heavenly Father—which is what Bill did every day as he pulled his wagon around the east side of St. Paul.

Many of us feel inadequate. We compare ourselves to others and conclude that we don't measure up. The media bombards us with what it means to be successful and important, but those definitions have everything to do with beauty, power, money, and position. By our world's definition, most of us are, like my son said of me, ordinary people.

Here is the irony: Jesus changed the rules about what constitutes "ordinary" and "significant." He told the wealthy and the powerful that without Him, their lives had no eternal significance. Then He told the poor and outcast that with Him, their lives had eternal meaning. Jesus viewed significance from an eternal perspective because we are eternal beings. Our significance comes not from what we do or have but from who we are—men and women made in God's image for relationship with Him and for joining Him in His work in this world.

Jesus infuses our lives with purpose and significance, and He asks that we live out the destiny He uniquely designed for us. By doing this—in our workplaces, neighborhoods, families, and churches—we become God's hands and feet and voice in a world that desperately needs hope and good news.

PURPOSE BRINGS PASSION

Understanding why God placed us on earth and the unique role He designed for us has a powerful influence on how we live our lives. Too many people live without clear direction, randomly moving from one thing to another, rather than living with intentional focus. Being able to answer the question posed in this chapter can radically change a random life into a focused life because we clearly understand how God wants us to contribute to His work.

Chris is one of the most hard-charging and success-driven people I have ever met. In college he became a millionaire by selling a version of those do-everything knives you see advertised on late-night television. He was young, rich, and full of himself. Since the real estate market was booming at the time, Chris considered real estate the best way to make his next million. He dumped his money into Dallas real estate, and his timing was perfect—for the perfect storm, that is. The market tanked and the young man who thought he was invincible lost everything. Chris found himself bagging groceries in a local supermarket.

Chris knew about God and was a Christ follower, but he was more interested in doing his own thing than God's thing. He lived a compromised Christian life that did not place Christ at the center. Instead, success was his god.

A few years later, on a trip to Asia, Chris fell in love with the place and decided to settle in Hong Kong. He started a furniture rental business, furnishing apartments for expatriates living across Asia. Again, his business began to expand—first across Asia, then into the Middle East, Africa, and Europe.

God, the relentless pursuer, kept knocking on Chris's door, but he was busy keeping his business afloat. Then one day Chris faced the truth that he was once again on the verge of bankruptcy. He looked around at the emptiness of his life and another crumbling business and knew that, whatever happened, he needed to renew his acquaintance with Jesus Christ.

Chris was a broken man. He understood that he was inadequate and that the pursuit of success could not be the ultimate purpose of life. Finding an international church in Hong Kong, he committed himself to following Christ no matter what the cost and began a mentoring relationship with the pastor.

Everything changed. Chris realized that his life had an eternal purpose—one far more important than chasing the next deal. He realized that his business was not really his, but God's, and that he was merely a steward of the Lord's resources. Finally, and most significantly, he understood his purpose in life: to spread the good news of Christ and to share the gospel with those he encountered.

An amazing thing happened. As Chris started to share his story with others, he saw all kinds of people choose to give their lives to Christ. He spoke to groups of people who didn't know God, and the same thing happened. As he began to use his business as a platform for sharing the gospel, he saw God bless his business. Today Chris is involved in both business and ministry. His life, talents, and resources are all directed toward helping people come to Christ. Having an eternal purpose changed everything for Chris.

Earlier I mentioned my hundred-year-old friend, Naomi. She lives in an assisted-care center with a group of folks who mostly live in confusion, having either given up on life or lost the use of their minds. For Naomi, whose mind is still as sharp as that of a fifty-year-old, the assisted-care center is not always an easy place to be.

Naomi understands that God created her to be an encourager of others and a prayer warrior on their behalf. Few people pray more regularly for me and others than Naomi does. She is committed to making a difference among those she lives with. Understanding her God-given purpose has turned what could be a seemingly pointless stage of life into one infused with meaning and significance.

The power of purpose changes how we deal with adversity and pain. Both are a part of everyone's life. Each life has either hidden or visible pain—no one is exempt. Adversity and pain bring with them discouragement and often cause people to pull into their shells and hunker down for the duration. I have met those who have allowed their pain to foster bitterness and hopelessness, and I have met others who have used their pain to build character and prompt new resolve. What makes the difference?

The difference is one of perspective: eternal perspective. We often are told that Jesus came to bring us a life of leisure, success, happiness, and prosperity. The truth is that Jesus promised a life of meaning, significance, forgiveness, and joy (in spite of circumstances). He did not promise that life would be easy, and He offered His life as an example. He said, "Anyone who does not take his cross and follow me is not worthy of me" (Matthew 10:38).

The cross is not a picture of luxury and ease but of faithfulness and suffering. The apostle Paul used battle metaphors to describe the spiritual realities of our world: "For our struggle is not against flesh and blood, but against the rulers, against the authorities, against the powers of this dark world and against the spiritual forces of evil in the heavenly realms" (Ephesians 6:12). When we engage in God's business, the evil one will engage in our business!

But if I am in the service of God and if He has given me a life mission, I can face adversity with a sense of honor (I am doing it for Him) and courage (He is always with me). After all, it is not about me; it's all about Him. Like any mission, our God-given one will include hardships, temporary defeats, pain, and struggle. We move forward on His behalf and refuse to be deterred by the discouragements along the way.

Knowing our purpose gives our lives focus. I believe that God placed me on this earth to build His church globally and make His Son look good. There are many things that I could do, but these are the central things God wants *me* to do. So I have oriented my life, time, energies, and gifts around this purpose.

We should not confuse the God-given purpose of our lives with our occupations. I said earlier that my wife, Mary Ann, is all about helping hurting people, loving the unloved, and extending God's mercy to those who need it. She has done that as a full-time housewife, as a high school nurse, and in various hospital settings. Her occupation has changed over the past thirty-three years of our marriage, but her unique kingdom assignment has not.

Our occupation may be directly related to our unique calling, or it may not be. The assignment God gives us is not necessarily related to our job or vocation. Rather, our occupation becomes one more platform from which we can be an influence for Christ.

OUR PURPOSE IS LINKED TO GOD'S PURPOSE

God has a plan for our world, and His plan is specifically related to His call on our lives. The ministry of Christ in dying for our sin is not simply about eternal life after our years on earth are done. Rather, God desires that our world be transformed by His people here and now. Consider these amazing words from the Lord's Prayer: "Our Father in heaven, hallowed be your name, *your kingdom come, your will be done on earth as it is in heaven*" (Matthew 6:9-10, emphasis added). Think about the implications of this prayer: "*Your* kingdom come, *your* will be done on earth as it is in heaven."

How is God's will done in heaven? Perfectly. There is no injustice, no sin, no lack of grace or mercy, no racism or devaluation of people, no illness or sadness. By using that prayer as our model, we are asking the Father to bring His perfect kingdom to our world, our neighborhoods, our inner cities, our workplaces, our schools, our police stations.

How can that happen in a corrupt, sinful, and selfish world? The answer is simple and profound. It happens bit by bit as those who follow Him are His hands, feet, heart, and words in the places we work and live. As we pursue our unique calling, we bring small bits of the perfect will of God to those around us. We are the answer as we live out the purpose He has for our lives, empowered by His Spirit.

When Christ returns to reign in person on a remade earth, His will shall be done perfectly on earth as it is in heaven, for heaven will merge with earth (see Revelation 21). In the meantime, our willingness to live out His purpose is a hopeful down payment on what is yet to come.

Our world has many sad situations like that of a "garbage village" about an hour outside of Cairo, Egypt. Those who live in the village are the garbage collectors for the nearby town. Daily they bring the garbage back to their hovels and dump it in their backyards. Think of your backyard full of hundreds of people's garbage and you get the picture. Add chickens and goats that feed on the rotting food. Then think of the parents and children who spend their days sorting through the garbage piles, living in the clothes they salvage, and playing with toys they find there, and the picture is more complete.

There are no bathrooms, running water, or electricity, and homes are nothing more than a few cinder blocks with some sheet metal for a roof. Furniture is whatever can be salvaged from the garbage. Streets are mud, and every year the village is flooded during the rainy season. If hell had a face, this would be hell.

That is, except for a Christ follower who has been working in the village for several years. He has built a school, a clinic, a basketball court, and a place for villagers to gather in a clean, safe environment. It is an oasis in an ocean of stinking garbage. On a regular basis, other Christian Egyptians come and lend support, help families build better dwellings, share the good news of Jesus, provide medical care, and try to help the children get an education so they can leave the cycle of grinding, dirty poverty.

In small but very real ways, this individual and those who support him bring a bit of heaven to a place of hell: changing lives, training kids, healing the sick, loving the outcast. I visited one of the families who has found the love of Jesus. The mother was holding a tiny baby in her arms. Despite the family's desperate plight, they have hope and smiles on their faces. They have an advocate both in Christ and in this man.

It is at the intersection of God's call on our lives and our willingness to embrace that call that His will happens on earth as it is already done in heaven. That is precisely what is happening in the garbage village. Through us, Jesus wants to permeate a sinful world with His wonderful mercy and love. We are not simply destined for heaven. Before we get there, it is our privilege to bring large and small bits of heaven to earth—and in the process show a hurting world the hope of Jesus Christ.

In calling us to His work, the Lord of the universe is inviting us to give up our small dreams and embrace the vast purpose that could have been designed only by Him. Jesus put it this way: "Whoever finds his life will lose it, and whoever loses his life for my sake will find it" (Matthew 10:39). Real life is found as God's purpose for our lives intersects with our embracing of that purpose. Anything else is merely existing.

THIS IS WHAT I WAS MADE FOR

There is a reason many people live with little satisfaction and inner peace. They have not discovered their purpose or do not know the One who created them for relationship with Him. The lie of the evil one is that we will be content and happy when we have everything we want and can do all that we desire. If that were true, all those who win big in the lottery would live happy, satisfied lives, when in fact the vast majority find themselves bankrupt and miserable. Our world has many successful individuals who have no real purpose in life other than to close the next deal. But that is an elusive goal, a moving target. They close the deal and then what?

Too often we have believed that life satisfaction comes from our income, our toys, our options, and our leisure pursuits. None of those are bad things, but they cannot lead us to the one thing our hearts so desperately long for: lasting satisfaction that comes from a life that counts for something permanent and transcendent.

Jesus often upends our assumptions, and He does so again on this one. Our life satisfaction has nothing to do with what we have. Instead, it has everything to do with who we know (Jesus) and understanding and living out His purposes (His work). This means that deep-down satisfaction is available to everyone, regardless of job, education, wealth, or status. All we need to do is embrace His call on our lives.

If you do not know what you were made for, you will have a much better idea as you work your way through this book. Finding the ten key pieces of the puzzle that allow you to make sense of the larger picture is a challenge, but it's not impossible. It takes an open heart and a willingness to ask and answer the ten crucial questions.

When I am using my vision, communication, or strategic gifts, I know and feel that "this is what I was made for!" It is what brings me the greatest joy, the most passion and fulfillment. I meet all kinds of people who live without passion or purpose. They have not figured out what they were made for. When people discover what God made them for, an amazing transformation takes place. It changes everything.

Much has been said in recent years about the joy of pursuing God; without a doubt there is no more important pursuit. However, we should never be fooled into thinking that our pursuit of God can be disconnected from joining Him in His work. God pursues us for relationship and assignment—these two cannot be disconnected from one another. Those who pursue Him also pursue His kingdom agenda and give their lives to His purposes.

It is in the fulfilling of our unique calling that we deepen our friendship with God, see our lives transformed, and develop His heart for the world. With this relationship comes a mission—the most important assignment we will ever have and one that leaves an eternal legacy.

CLARIFYING YOUR UNIQUE PURPOSE

How can we gain clarity in answering the "Why am I here?" question? I have five suggestions:

First, ask God to reveal to you what His unique assignment is. He created you to join Him in His work. Start to ask Him regularly to reveal His custom-tailored mission to you.

Second, ask those who know you best how they would answer that question for you based on the strengths, interests, and aptitudes they observe in your life. Others often see in us what we do not see in ourselves. Write down your friends' answers and ponder them with an open heart and mind.

Third, reflect on how God has used you in the past and how He is using you now. Are there clues about how God has gifted you?

Fourth, think about opportunities you have had to bring a little bit of heaven to someone or to some situation in your circle of influence. In your journal or a notebook, list some of those times and places where you embraced His call on your life. Identifying the ways you have influenced others will provide clear direction in understanding your God-given assignment.

Lastly, based on what you currently know, complete the following sentence: "God has placed me on this earth in order to . . ." You may not have a final, conclusive answer, but it's helpful to put into words what you believe God is calling you to do.

God created each of us for a special purpose, so the most important thing we can do is prayerfully identify that purpose and begin living it out. The alternative is to focus our lives on the common, temporal indicators of success: status, possessions, recreation, and all that is defined as "the good life." But in the end we miss the most important reason

God placed us here. True greatness and satisfaction come as we fulfill our divine mandate.

REFLECTIVE PRAYER

Father, I thank You that my life has eternal meaning. I thank You that You created me for relationship with You and work for You. I am amazed that You would choose to have me join You in Your work. Reveal to me what my unique role is and then release me to do that work with great freedom and joy. I want to live at the intersection of Your call and my willingness to embrace that call. Amen.

For Group Discussion

- Share how you completed the following sentence: "God has placed me on this earth in order to . . ." Then provide feedback to one another.
- How do the truths of Ephesians 2:10 influence how you see and live your life? What would you like to do differently?
- What is the correlation between being made for relationship with Christ and working for Christ? What happens when one of these gets out of balance?
- Where have you seen people bringing little bits of heaven to earth this week?
- What do you think are the greatest barriers to Christ followers living out the call of God on their lives?

Chapter 2

WHAT IS MY SWEET SPOT?

UNDERSTANDING HOW YOU'RE WIRED

We have different gifts, according to the grace given us.

— ROMANS 12:6

Have you ever watched people who are amazingly good at something and thought, *How do they do that?*

I think of Corbyn, a videographer who can tell a story that grips the heart every time he makes a film. He is brilliant at translating a concept into film in a way that is captivating and compelling. I see his work and wish I had that kind of creativity.

Thankfully, there are a few things I do that make me pause and say, "I was made for this. I know God gave me gifts in this area." I imagine that you, too, can point to those areas in your life where the gifts flow as naturally as water from a spring. You know you are in your sweet spot. When we are in our zone of gifting, we feel fulfilled, challenged, and satisfied. It's a great place to be.

When God reveals His unique work for us and asks us to participate with Him, He also gives us what we need to accomplish our mission. He never asks us to do something He does not equip us to do—although He may ask us to do things we *think* we're not capable of doing. (If we could do something based on our own abilities, it would not be a God-sized assignment.) He asks us to do things that stretch us, maybe even scare us, and then He provides the ability to pull it off. He has intentionally wired us for the work for which He created us.

Moses discovered this truth when God rocked his world at the burning bush (see Exodus 3). God was going to rescue His people from bondage, and He told Moses he was the one to lead the people out of Egypt. This didn't make Moses' day. He responded with fear and a list of reasons why he was the wrong guy for the job.

Moses said what we often feel: "Who am I, that I should go to Pharaoh and bring the Israelites out of Egypt?" (3:11). Have you ever felt that way when asked to take on some responsibility? When we ask, "Who am I?" we are really saying, "I'm not qualified. This deal is too big for me."

God's response was simple and straightforward: "I will be with you" (3:12). That is what God wants you and me to hear as well. *I will be with you.* We are not alone in pursuing God's mission for us. If the God of the universe is with us, why should we be afraid?

But Moses was not done pushing back. He said, "O LORD, I have never been eloquent, neither in the past nor since you have spoken to your servant. I am slow of speech and tongue" (4:10).

The Lord responded by saying, "Who gave man his mouth? Who makes him deaf or mute? Who gives him sight or makes him blind? Is it not I, the LORD? Now go; I will help you speak and will teach you what to say" (4:11-12).

Moses essentially complained, "God, I don't have the ability or gifts to do what You are asking me to do." And God responded, "Excuse Me? You say you have a problem speaking, but are you not talking to the One who gives man the very ability to speak?"

God invites us to live at the intersection of His call and our willingness to embrace His call. In responding, we fulfill the unique and special work that God designed just for us. As we are faithful in fulfilling His purpose for our lives, we bring His hope into the corners of the world we inhabit and into the circles of influence we have.

The apostle Paul told us in Ephesians 2:10 that each of us is a work of art created by God—and works of art are always unique. As we saw in the last chapter, the work He has for each of us is also unique. When we understand our unique wiring—our gifts, talents, strengths—we better understand God's call on our lives and how He desires us to help change the world.

In our church programs today we tend to fill ministry slots with any available body. But this approach leads to frustration and ineffectiveness. What we should do first is look at how God has uniquely wired individuals and then find opportunities for ministry that are consistent with their unique wiring.

Some people are doers; they want a project to attack. Some are thinkers who want to figure something out. Some are detail oriented and enjoy administrative tasks, while others hate details and want to strategize the big picture. Some are wired to lead, and others are wired to work as part of a team. Some love to be up front while others prefer to serve behind the scenes.

When we live, work, and minister in our sweet spot—honoring the way God has wired us—we are most fulfilled and fruitful. When we don't, we experience frustration. Our strengths and abilities were divinely implanted by the Father so we can fulfill our unique role and build an eternal legacy.

OUR UNIQUE WIRING

I am constantly amazed at how different my two sons are. Jon, my eldest, is by nature quiet, self-assured, analytical, and serious. He is currently completing a triple major in economics, business, and philosophy. I sometimes describe him as "my son who suffers from thinking too deeply." He prefers to have a few very close friends, to whom he is fiercely loyal.

Steven, on the other hand, is highly creative. He is a visual learner who has the ability to design something in his head, put it on paper, and then make it—whether with his forge, wood tools, or sewing machine. What's more, he is a "people magnet"—the kids he serves and works with will follow him anywhere.

Our unique wiring is not an accident. It goes back to the central truth of this book that "we are God's workmanship, created in Christ Jesus to do good works, which God prepared in advance for us to do" (Ephesians 2:10). Every one of us is wired by God for the work He created us to do.

This fits with the New Testament teaching that each of us has been given spiritual gifts by the Father to use on His behalf. Our spiritual gifts are closely interwoven with our unique wiring. If you take a spiritual gift inventory along with a secular gift inventory (such as StrengthsFinder[1]), you will find a remarkable similarity. Of course, it is when we become a part of God's family that these gifts are empowered by the Holy Spirit, sometimes taking us to new levels of ability to accomplish His work.

When I was young, I was pretty sure I had lots of strengths. Ah, the foolishness of youth! Today I know that I have a few strong gifts, and everything left over is a weakness. The fact that each of us has a few strong areas and most everything else is a weakness has been demonstrated time and again by research and testing in the marketplace. Conventional wisdom once said that we should work hard to turn our weaknesses into strengths. We now know that while we can minimize a weakness, it will never be a strength. So the trick is to understand as best we can how God has wired us — where He has given us special ability — and work on honing and improving those areas.

I love watching people to figure out how they are wired. I think of Mark, the directional leader of Heartland Community Church in Rockford, Illinois. He puts together strategic ministry plans that others believe impossible and leverages those plans for huge ministry undertakings. Once a successful investor, Mark now uses his skills to scope out ministry opportunities that others don't see. He initiates and manages ministry portfolios just as he once put together financial portfolios.

Eric, also with Heartland Community Church, is a codeveloper of one of the most innovative, customized spiritual-formation tools to be introduced to the church.[2] He is a CPA by training and was an analyst for a commodities trading company. Now he's using his analytical skills to think outside the traditional box in order to help men and women everywhere grow in Christ. Eric is going to change the lives of hundreds of thousands of people because he is using his wiring for the building of the kingdom.

When I meet frustrated, tired, and depleted people, I ask whether they are working and ministering in their areas of strength. Are there many things they do that drain rather than energize them? Any of us can migrate out of the zone of our strengths and wake up one day wondering why we are unhappy and unfulfilled. This is why we must understand how we are wired and what our strengths are. The more we operate out of our strengths, the more effective we will be and the more happiness we will experience.

GETTING CLARITY ON WIRING

Understanding our skills and strengths allows us to utilize them for our most effective work. Several questions can help us determine how we are wired:

- What things fill my tank and what things deplete me? For example, I love to write; it fills my tank, which is a clue that it may be a strength. On the other hand, I don't like administrative work, so that's a clue that it is not a strength.
- What things do I love to do and what do I put off? As I write this, I am putting off some of those administrative tasks (another clue).
- At what activities am I most effective — and at what am I either marginally effective or really poor? God wired and gifted us to be effective. If we are only marginally effective or downright lousy at something, it is not in our strength set.
- How would I design my ideal job description or role in life? The answer to that question is a clue to how you are wired if it is consistent with your answers to the other questions.
- How do others evaluate my areas of strength and weakness? This is a helpful question because sometimes we think we are great at something, while others would disagree. Objective feedback from those who know us well provides valuable insight.

- If I could change one thing about my current job or role that would make me more fulfilled, what would it be? What we normally want to change is either to get out of an area of weakness or into an area of strength.
- In areas of ministry, what do I gravitate toward and where have I made the most significant contributions? For me it is in designing ministry strategy, writing, and speaking.
- What are the things that I would be willing to spend my day off doing because I love it so much? Give me a day off and you will find me reading, writing, or fly-fishing.
- Who are my heroes and role models? Often, those we look up to are people who have similar wirings. My favorite historical figure is Winston Churchill, who embodies something I care deeply about: effective leadership.
- What is my life verse? Often our life verse reflects what we are passionate about and gifted for. Mine is Ephesians 4:12, which is all about helping people to join God in His work.
- What kinds of books do I like to read? I most enjoy books on leadership and biographies of leaders because leadership is one of my strengths.
- What have I learned about myself from tests I have taken? The StrengthsFinder test tells me that my top five strengths are Maximizer, Strategic, Achiever, Relator, and Input.

Sometimes we have only a partial view of our wiring, which over time becomes more complete. When I was in high school, I believed my career would be centered on teaching and writing. What I did not envision was the leadership component of my wiring that has always been a part of my various roles. Today, I would define my strengths as leadership, vision/strategy, and communication. Almost everything else is not a strength of mine.

The advantage of understanding how God has wired us is that we no longer need to feel bad about those things we are not good at. I am confident God wired me the way He did for good reasons, and I do not feel guilty about the things I don't do well (although I must be careful not to use this as an excuse to avoid working on my weaknesses). We should not look at others and wish we could do what they can do. After all, we each have our own God-given strengths.

STRENGTHS AND VOCATION

It is an added blessing when what we do for a living is in our sweet spot. This is not always possible since sometimes we just need a job to pay the bills. And when we're young, we don't always know what our strengths are—it takes some trial and error to figure them out. But if you are deeply dissatisfied with your occupation or job and don't feel that it aligns with who God made you to be, consider making it a matter of prayer and exploration. The more closely your strengths and vocation are aligned, the happier and more effective you will be.

I have met people who are in vocations they have known for years they were not made for. Sometimes it is because their parents had a plan for their life that was not consistent with their unique gifting and wiring as an adult. If this is your situation, don't simply settle for less. Prayerfully consider moving in a direction that would bring you greater joy and satisfaction.

Tim was a successful stockbroker for most of his career, but he never wanted to do that. His heart had always longed to be in ministry, but early in his life others convinced him that making money should be a top priority. For decades he achieved financial success . . . and felt deeply unhappy. Finally, in his early fifties, he quit his brokerage job and went to work for a nonprofit ministry using his financial and sales skills to develop relationships and raise funds. For the first time, his heart, passion, and skills were in alignment and his contentment level was high.

If you believe your vocation is not aligned with how God wired you, would you be willing to take the risk to try something different? Even if it means a drop in income, it is a wonderful, fulfilling thing to work from areas of passion, strength, and satisfaction.

STRENGTHS AND MARRIAGE

I wonder how much conflict might be avoided if we paid attention to strengths and sweet spots in our marriages. For years, my wife took care of the household finances, but it was a major source of anxiety for her—a clue that this was not her sweet spot. When I took over that responsibility, she relaxed noticeably.

Sometimes there is conflict around strengths or lack of them. I grew up in a home where everything was always picked up and in order, the house was vacuumed and dusted, and beds were made—before school in the morning. Sure, there were ten kids to get it done, but also ten kids to mess up the house in the first place. For that many people living under one roof, our house was amazingly orderly and uncluttered.

For the first years of our marriage, the contrast between my growing-up home and my new home was a source of conflict and frustration. Finally I decided that it didn't matter that my mother's values and strengths were different from Mary Ann's. (Now, we don't live in a messy house, just a more lived-in house.) Given the choice of spending time on housework or helping someone in need, Mary Ann will choose the latter every time. Which is better? For her, the answer is simple: helping people!

Understanding the way you and your spouse are wired and utilizing one another's strengths contributes greatly to a happy marriage. Many times a spouse is not encouraged to celebrate his or her unique gifting and to fully put those strengths to good use. This is a tragedy because it dishonors him or her, who is made in the image of God and has a unique and special role to play in the kingdom. In marriage, let's work hard to recognize, embrace, and champion our spouse's gifts for the glory of God.

STRENGTHS AND MINISTRY

It is also important that we pay attention to God's gifting when we consider what ministries or community services we devote our time to. My friend Ken, a businessman, is one of the most insightful thinkers I know. He regularly serves on ministry boards because doing so provides the opportunity to leverage his strengths for the kingdom.

Betty is a natural networker, the consummate connector of people. She has the ability to befriend anyone, discern his or her spiritual gifts, determine needs and desires, and connect that person to the right small group or outreach project. Her husband, Ron, has the gift of seeing things that need to be done around the church—and he gets them done. He is one of those quiet behind-the-scenes servants who "greases the wheels" for effective ministry.

There may be seasons in which we intentionally choose to take on responsibilities outside our strength sets simply because they need to be done. However, we should invest the bulk of our time in areas where God has gifted us so that we maximize our impact. Most of my wife's ministry takes place outside the church as she meets needs in the neighborhood or at work. Because she's already using her gifts, it's okay for her to say no to requests that are outside of her gift set. Even Jesus on occasion said no to things that God had not called Him to do. It is a "positive no" because, by saying no to some good things, we are able to invest our time and talents in things that better utilize our strengths.

This is a matter of stewardship. When I say yes to things that are not in my gift set, I will not be nearly as effective and energized as when I say yes to those that are aligned with my gifts.

Do not confuse "ministry" with "church" here. While we should use our gifting in the church, we are also to use our gifts with those who are not yet in the body of Christ. Many of us will have our most profound impact in our neighborhoods, workplaces, or peer groups. God's intention is that His will is done on earth as it is in heaven. He wants us to bring His values, character, and truth to all the places we frequent—and most of those are outside our churches. Jesus wants His kingdom to come to our world, not just to the confines of our places of worship.

I believe that much depression, discontent, and unhappiness revolve around the fact that individuals are not working, serving, or ministering in their areas of strength. They fail to realize the spiritual dynamic at work. God made all of us for a purpose and then wired us a special way to help accomplish His purpose. We will feel truly content only when we are fully engaging our strengths.

AFFIRMING AND APPRECIATING OTHERS' STRENGTHS

Many people have never had someone else say to them, "Wow, you are really good at that." Or "When you did that, you really made a difference." God has gifted everyone, but those gifts have often not been acknowledged or affirmed, especially when they're not the visible, up-front kind.

My friend Ron specializes in getting things done without any fuss or fanfare. He is exceptional at what he does, and he uses his gifts for Jesus. My hundred-year-old friend, Naomi, prays for me probably more than anyone else. But she does it quietly, putting her gift of faith to work on my behalf.

At the end of the apostle Paul's letters, he often sent greetings to specific people and affirmed something they had done. Most of these people are unknowns to us, but Paul understood that there are no insignificant people in God's eyes and that everyone's contribution is important if we are going to represent Christ in our world.

Who are the "unknowns" in your sphere, the people who don't get much recognition but who are faithfully using their gifts to serve Christ? How can you affirm and encourage them? The more we recognize and encourage those who are using their strengths and gifts, the more they will be motivated to use them. Encouragement is a powerful gift we can give to others.

A great deal of misunderstanding between people results from not appreciating the strengths of others. This is true in marriages, in churches, between friends, and at work. The first missionaries sent out from the early church were Paul and Barnabas. They could not have been more different. Paul was a headstrong, type A personality who was very mission driven. Barnabas was more patient, laid back, and relational. His name literally means "encourager." On one of their trips, a fellow named John Mark went along and somehow ticked Paul off—to the extent that on his next trip, Paul refused to take John Mark along.

Barnabas, being the peacemaker and encourager, strongly disagreed with Paul. He wanted to give John Mark another chance. Their disagreement was so intense that Barnabas and Paul went their separate ways (see Acts 15:36-41). They didn't appreciate one another's wiring, but thankfully they made peace later in life.

The uniqueness of human beings is intriguing. God's creativity is evident in every individual — each one is different and a bit quirky perhaps, with the potential to make an eternal difference. It is not by accident that when God designed church leadership, He formed a team (overseers or elders). When a ministry was needed to care for the widows in the early church, they chose a team (deacons). When the first missionaries were commissioned, they sent a team (Paul and Barnabas). When subsequent missionaries were sent out, they went in teams.

God prefers to utilize teams because He knows we all have a few strengths and a lot of weaknesses. In doing ministry together, we complement each other's assets and compensate for each other's liabilities. We live in an individualistic culture; when we are lone rangers doing our own thing, we miss out on the power of multiple gifts blending together in complementary teamwork.

A TEAM AND B TEAM?

A great hindrance to the gospel's influence in society today is the thinking that God has an A team and a B team. The A team members are those in full-time ministry who have Bible or seminary degrees. They are the ones qualified to really use their gifts in ministry. The rest are on the B team, helpful but not nearly as qualified or talented.

Think about this: When Paul wrote that *all of us* are gifted by the Holy Spirit and that *everyone's* contribution is equally needed, there were no Christian seminaries and very few full-time Christian workers. There was never to be an A team and a B team — just God's team.

A tragic trend today is the professionalization of ministry. Rather than unleashing all of God's people to influence the world, we often hire professionals and expect them to do it all for us. We have a generation of Christ followers who feel unqualified to get off the bench and into the game because they don't have formal theological training.

My life verses are Ephesians 4:11-12: "It was [Jesus] who gave some to be apostles, some to be prophets, some to be evangelists, and some to be pastors and teachers, to prepare God's people for works of service, so that the body of Christ may be built up." The role of those called into vocational ministry is not to do the ministry on behalf of others but to develop, empower, and release all of God's people into active, meaningful ministry in line with their giftings. There is nothing more powerful on the face of the earth than *all* of His people actively using the gifts He gave us.

God's strategy for reaching our communities is not that people would come to church find Him (though it's nice when that happens); His strategy is for us to go find them and demonstrate grace, love, and care — to "be Jesus" to them. That happens when we intentionally use our gifts in the church and in the world.

My father was a surgeon. In the hospital hierarchy, surgeons rank right up there near the top. But Dad never bought into that system and made it a point to honor everyone he came in contact with. Years after Dad retired, I was in the security line at the airport. The TSA agent looked at my license and ticket and asked, "Are you related to Dr. Addington, the surgeon?" I told him I was. He pressed further: "You mean Dr. Gordon Addington?" I acknowledged that he was my dad. The agent then said, "Your dad befriended me when I was a janitor at United Hospital and even invited me over for Christmas one year." The man was obviously moved and influenced by this simple gesture. Dad's intentionality in showing this gentleman dignity and friendship when he was at the bottom of the hospital-staff hierarchy made an impact on this man.

During the time I spent in United Hospital over the past year, I met a lot of folks who asked, "Are you related to Dr. Addington?" They proceeded to tell me how Dad had befriended them when they were colleagues. Dad simply brought the values, truth, and character of Christ into that place. As Jesus said, "Your kingdom come, your will be done on earth as it is in heaven." That's what Dad was doing.

You are on God's team, and as you use your gifts in the church, community, workplace, and neighborhood, you are Christ to those who may only meet Him through you. God never intended for only those who serve as full-time Christian workers to accomplish His work on earth. He intended for *everyone* who follows Him to be part of that divine work.

THE BOTTOM LINE

It is God's plan and intention that the gospel change the world — that the righteousness of heaven actually affect how things are done on earth now! And it happens in small ways every day, all over our planet, when God's people use the strengths He has given and empowered them to use.

One person may help a hurting child. Another may offer words of encouragement to everyone she meets. Another may volunteer with the homeless. Multiply those activities by each believer using his or her gifts, and we'll offer far more than a "thousand points of light."[3] We will have millions of pieces of heaven showing up here on earth, which all contribute to the work God designed for us and the legacy He wants us to have.

I encourage you to spend time thinking about your unique God-given gifts. Write down in your journal or a notebook what you believe your key strengths are. Where are you able to use your wiring, gifting, and strengths inside and outside of the church?

REFLECTIVE PRAYER

Father, thank You for gifting me with strengths that I can use to advance Your work in this world. Give me understanding as to how You have wired me and how I can use my unique gifting to serve You and others. Amen.

For Group Discussion

- Share your thoughts about how God has uniquely wired you and the strengths He has given you. Receive feedback from the rest of the group.
- How are you presently able to use your gifting both among God's people and in the world

where He has placed you? Where have you experienced God's empowerment for a specific ministry?

- As a result of reading this chapter, have you thought of new areas in which you may be especially wired or gifted to serve?
- Have you ever experienced the "Moses syndrome" — fearful and insecure to the point that you want to run from God's assignment? How did you resolve the situation? What's the best response when we encounter times like this?
- How specifically can you affirm the gifts of others this week?

Chapter 3

WHAT WILL I LEAVE BEHIND?

Looking Toward Your Legacy

I have fought the good fight, I have finished the race, I have kept the faith. Now there is in store for me the crown of righteousness, which the Lord, the righteous Judge, will award to me on that day—and not only to me, but also to all who have longed for his appearing.

— 2 Timothy 4:7-8

What if you could shape the legacy you leave? Randy Pausch, a professor at Carnegie Mellon, had that opportunity when he was diagnosed with terminal pancreatic cancer. Millions have been influenced by "The Last Lecture" he gave on lessons he had learned in his life. His book *The Last Lecture*[1] was his way of passing along his wisdom to the public and especially to the three children he left behind.

The courage and grace with which Randy and his wife, Jai, faced his terminal diagnosis inspired those who watched his television interviews. His book caused people to think about the power of legacy and what they will leave behind.

Final words are powerful—as are the values, commitments, actions, and priorities with which we live our lives. We may not have the opportunity to give a last lecture that sums up the lessons we've learned, but each of us leaves a legacy that affects those we leave behind . . . and take with us into eternity.

For each of us, our life has a finish line. The question is, When we reach that line, what will we leave behind? What legacy will we leave?

When I consult with organizations on issues like their preferred future, we never start with the present. Rather, we ask, "What do you want to look like in ten years? What kind of organization do you want to be and what impact do you want to have?" We first look at the desired end result and then design a plan that will make it possible for the organization to reach its target.

As individuals, we often live life without much of a target. We respond to the demands of the moment, the job, the expectations of others, and the overwhelming busyness of life. But too many people get to the finish line with a long list of regrets.

We realize we didn't invest enough time in our children or marriage. We're sorry we did not have more time for deep relationships. We wish there had been more time for reflection and thinking. Now there is too little time for those things that suddenly are more important than the salary we pulled down or the ladder we climbed.

But here's the good news: It is possible to minimize the number of regrets we have at the finish line by determining *now* what we want our legacy to be. Then we can use that vision to create a blueprint for how we will live our lives today. In other words, we start with the end result we want and then arrange our lives in a way that is most likely to get us there.

God did not design life to be randomly or carelessly lived. He created us to be in relationship with Him and to join in His work in our world. There is purpose to our lives—eternal purpose that will outlive our days on this earth. None of us wants to get to the end of our life and realize we invested in the wrong things and expended our efforts on things that don't have lasting value.

Near the end of His life, Jesus said something significant: "I have brought you glory on earth by completing the work you gave me to do"

(John 17:4). He understood His purpose, had been faithful to it, and brought glory to His Father.

The apostle Paul said something similar near the end of his life:

> I have fought the good fight, I have finished the race, I have kept the faith. Now there is in store for me the crown of righteousness, which the Lord, the righteous Judge, will award to me on that day—and not only to me, but also to all who have longed for his appearing. (2 Timothy 4:7-8)

Paul's goal was to please Jesus with his life and enter eternity with Christ, knowing he had fulfilled God's unique work for him. He stayed engaged and faithful to the end, desiring to hear the words of the master from the parable of the talents, "Well done, good and faithful servant!" (Matthew 25:21).

What a legacy to leave! Don't you want to know at the end of your life that you have lived well, stayed engaged with Christ, who made you for relationship, and completed the work He uniquely gifted you to do? That is our challenge. You might be thinking to yourself, *This sounds hard!* Not really. Because when you understand why you are here, what you are made to do, and how you can utilize your gifts to accomplish it, your legacy will be the natural result.

As a NASCAR fan, I love to watch a good race. The best drivers are great "drafters." They keep their car almost bumper to bumper behind the car in front of them, taking advantage of the aerodynamic draft that carries them along. Living out our legacy is all about drafting closely behind Christ in the work He designed for us, allowing Him to carry us along as we live in our passion and stay empowered by His Spirit.

Here is the equation: As I live out the work God designed for me, in line with how God wired me, I will leave a wonderful legacy. God didn't make it hard. He specifically equipped me to do what He called me to do, and as I do it, I leave an eternal legacy. I encourage you to claim it as your own.

INVESTING TALENTS TO ENSURE GAIN

Jesus' parable of the talents (see Matthew 25) is all about living in such a way that we leave a legacy. In the parable, the master calls his three servants and tells them he is going on a long journey. He divides up his wealth and tells the servants to invest it well so there is an increase when he returns.

Later, when he comes back, the master finds that two of the servants have doubled the money he gave them to manage. To these two, the master says, "Well done, good and faithful servant! You have been faithful with a few things; I will put you in charge of many things. Come and share your master's happiness!" (verse 21).

But the third servant was preoccupied with his own life and didn't have time for his master's investments. He simply buried the money and offered a lame excuse for why he had not invested it on his master's behalf. He thought life was about him rather than about his master. The master's words for the third servant were harsh:

> You wicked, lazy servant! So you knew that I harvest where I have not sown and gather where I have not scattered seed? Well then, you should have put my money on deposit with the bankers, so that when I returned I would have received it back with interest.
>
> Take the talent from him and give it to the one who has the ten talents. For everyone who has will be given more, and he will have an abundance. Whoever does not have, even what he has will be taken from him. And throw that worthless servant outside, into the darkness, where there will be weeping and gnashing of teeth. (verses 26-30)

There is a message of blessing and warning in this parable. The master represents Christ, and the servants represent us. The money the master handed out is the gifts, opportunities, and unique work Christ has given us to accomplish on His behalf. We choose whether we will faithfully manage what He has entrusted or live a life of preoccupation and selfishness. Will we be like the first two servants, who took their steward-ship seriously, or like the third, who took only his self-interests seriously?

The amazing thing is that Jesus entrusts to each of us a portion of His ministry. He gifts us with abilities and empowers us with His Spirit. We have been invited by the Lord of the universe to represent Him and make a difference for His kingdom by bringing hope to our needy planet. This is one of the greatest blessings we could experience because these invest-ments have eternal value.

But there is also a warning in the parable of the talents. Some people are so consumed with their own stuff that, like the unfaithful servant, they bury the talents and ignore the responsibility God gives. When they cross the finish line, they will have little to show for their lives. They will have squandered the opportunity to infuse their world with God's love, and they will leave little eternal legacy.

The unfaithful servant exemplifies a wasted life that might have enjoyed temporal success but was an eternal failure. In the end, it is a life of deep regret. The unfaithful servant chose to do his own thing and in the process lost the joy and satisfaction that the other two servants experienced.

Take a moment to thoughtfully list in your journal or a notebook the areas of life you know are critical if you are going to leave a healthy legacy. Next, give yourself a grade for how you are currently doing in fulfilling your legacy. Be honest. The purpose of this is not to create guilt; we have enough of that in our lives. It is to recognize that if we are going to reach the finish line as we want to, we must give immediate attention to what is ultimately important. Either we pay attention now or we experience deep regret later.

You may say, "But it's too late for me." It is never too late to pay atten-tion to what is important. In fact, as long as we have life and breath, we have opportunity to create a meaningful legacy. God's grace covers our past, and He calls us to follow Him today into the future.

TO THE YOUNG

A great joy of my life is to mentor young people and help them figure out how God has wired them, how they can grow their relationship with Jesus, and how they can make a difference in this world. If you are in the early years of life, don't think this discussion about legacy is not for you. The sooner you understand how God wants to use you and start intentionally using your gifts for Him, the more joyful and purposeful your life will be.

This morning I spent an hour via the Internet with Chad, who is in his twenties. A former professional skateboarder, he is a creative type who cares deeply for people. Like many his age, he is passionate about Jesus and just needs encouragement to go for it and put his talents to good use.

When I asked Chad why God made him, he replied, "To make a difference with hurting, poor, and suffering people." Chad does not know what vocation he will ultimately have. But whatever his career ends up being, he already has a glimpse of the calling of God on his life.

The world belongs to the young. You will shape the future of society and ministry. Your passion and influence and ministry count! Take the baton that Jesus hands you and help change the world into what God created it to be. Your desire for genuine community, compassion ministries, authenticity, equality, and justice are values our world desperately needs.

Every time you challenge the status quo and fight for justice, every time you show compassion and provide help to the hurting, every time you show honor to the marginalized, every time you knock down walls of racism or seek to alleviate poverty, you are fulfilling the Lord's Prayer: "Your kingdom come, your will be done on earth as it is in heaven." Your active engagement in living out the values and priorities of Jesus' kingdom will help bring God's perfect will to an imperfect world.

Jon and Mandy were living in a quiet Wisconsin town when Hurricane Katrina smashed into New Orleans and a call was put out for volunteers to help rebuild homes and lives. They felt God saying, "That job is for you." So they made a six-month commitment, packed up their kids, and headed for New Orleans. Six months later they returned to Wisconsin and sold the dream home Jon had built, knowing that God wanted them to stay in New Orleans.

For two years they lived on a shoestring budget, working with hundreds of volunteers each month to gut and rebuild homes—at no cost to the homeowners. In those two years they worked with more than ten thousand volunteers and rebuilt scores of homes. They saw lives change each week—the lives of folks in Louisiana who were helped and the lives of volunteers who went home eager to do holistic ministry in their own communities. Jon and Mandy's own lives were dramatically changed. They took the risk of living at the intersection of God's call and their own giftedness, and they will never be the same.

OPPORTUNITIES AND DANGERS OF "HALFTIME"

"Halftime" presents a great opportunity and also a major danger zone. Almost everyone who does not finish well fails in the second half of life. There are many who, like in the parable of the sower, allow their passion for God to be "choked by life's worries, riches and pleasures, and they do not mature" or live out their potential (Luke 8:14). They cannot say with Paul, "I have finished the race, I have kept the faith" (2 Timothy 4:7).

In the second half of life we can use the opportunity God gives us, like the first two servants in the parable of the talents, or we can bury our opportunity, like the third. We can answer God's call or choose to disregard it. Halftime is decision time. We can use the experiences, giftings, financial stability, and increased expendable time for His purposes, or we can focus instead on ourselves, allowing our passion for Jesus and His work to grow cold. The legacy we desire to leave can be lost if we do not stay focused during the second half.

Many of my heroes are people whose passion to know Christ and be used by Him grows as the years pass. These people want to finish well and leave an eternal legacy. We may retire from our jobs, but there is no retirement from the call of God on our lives or the work He created especially for us. As long as God does not retire from ministering to us, why would we retire from ministering for Him?

Those who feel they have "done their time" misunderstand the nature of God's call. Jobs are temporary; they come and go, and at a certain age most of us retire. God's calling is a *claim* on our lives, and from the time we make Him Lord we fully belong to Him. God's intention to infect our world with His love, care, mercy, forgiveness, truth, and justice happens as all of His children are actively involved in what He calls us to do. Every unengaged Christ follower leaves a hole in God's intentions for our world.

TRANSFORMING PAIN INTO LEGACY

Many reading this book have endured significant pain in their lives—pain inflicted by others, by life, and by themselves. This is what I want you to know: Pain, while never welcome, can be part of a wonderful legacy if properly channeled.

I had the sorrow of watching one of my heroes, Doug, wither away from ALS (Lou Gehrig's disease) over the past several years. He reached his finish line in February 2008. Doug was at the height of his business success when he received news of his disease. There was nothing fair about the disease he had to endure. Nor was it easy.

Yet throughout his journey with this disease, Doug demonstrated a grace, dignity, and faith that can only be a result of the Holy Spirit's work. He touched everyone he knew. Doug taught me a lot in the times we spent together, particularly about what it is to remain faithful during hardship.

God has a way of redeeming pain for His glory. I went through deep pain—the dark night of the soul—early in my career. It took years for my heart to fully recover. Yet through the pain, I understood God's grace in a new way. I developed empathy for others who were hurting, and the experience led me to help churches develop healthier leadership boards and ministries.

My future ministry was influenced by that pain, which God

graciously redeemed and used for His good. There is nothing that happens in our lives that God cannot turn into something useful. This is the wonderful nature of grace—even when we are responsible for our own pain. God has the power to turn what is hurtful into something helpful. The scars of deep pain have become a major part of my legacy, and through my consulting with church leaders, my scars have helped prevent others from bearing the same wounds.

The apostle Peter reminded us that our pain comes so that our "faith—of greater worth than gold, which perishes even though refined by fire—may be proved genuine and may result in praise, glory and honor when Jesus Christ is revealed" (1 Peter 1:7). The pain we suffer changes us and contributes to a legacy that grows even greater because of it.

Ann, a longtime friend, is a cancer survivor who has walked through some very tough years. She described her pain this way in a note to me:

> My life in the past three years shows a long series of dramatic "stones of remembrance" of God's faithfulness and grace. Grace has become my theme. As I look back, I see how God's used heartache, disappointment, disease, and even my sin to accomplish His glorious purposes in my life. I certainly don't deserve His goodness and favor, but He has lavished it upon me.

Pain is a reality of life. How we choose to respond to it will determine whether it contributes to our legacy. We can allow the experience to deepen our faith and increase our capacity to empathize with others. The alternative is to allow pain to detract from our legacy through bitterness or the inability to move beyond the hurt. If you find yourself trapped by pain, I urge you to get help because it will be a prison for you until you are able to place it in perspective. Learn from your pain and allow it to be a part of your history that positively informs your present and future.

It is in the difficult periods of life that we are most powerfully shaped and our character is most profoundly formed. This was true for Jesus as well. The writer of Hebrews said,

During the days of Jesus' life on earth, he offered up prayers and petitions with loud cries and tears to the one who could save him from death, and he was heard because of his reverent submission. Although he was a son, he learned obedience from what he suffered and, once made perfect, he became the source of eternal salvation for all who obey him. (5:7-9)

Pain is a friend, not an enemy, when seen from this perspective. I have walked through intense periods of pain—physical, emotional, relational, and professional. As I look back over my fifty-some years, I see how those periods were major factors in shaping who I have become and the impact I can have. My legacy has been shaped through pain and difficulty. In that light it has been a great gift. There is no pain that God cannot redeem for His glory.

Even this book came about as a result of pain. On December 4, 2007, I woke up unable to breathe. Mary Ann took me to the emergency room, which was the start of a forty-two-day hospital stay, thirty-two of them in the intensive care unit (ICU) and eighteen or so in a coma and on a ventilator.

It took a week for the doctors to discover that I had MRSA pneumonia (also known as methicillin-resistant Staphylococcus aureus). On my admission I had only 30 percent lung capacity and was in congestive heart failure. My days in the ICU were spent largely a heartbeat away from death, including complications of ARDS (acute respiratory distress syndrome), septic shock, a failed mitral valve, high fever, and atrial fibrillation (my heartbeat went up to 240 beats per minute). By everyone's analysis, I should *never* have left the hospital alive.

MRSA is often carried by individuals on their skin, but when it gets into the bloodstream, it is often fatal. Three days before I entered the hospital, I had had a tooth pulled, and it is speculated this is when MRSA entered my bloodstream. It turned out to be one of the worst possible strains, with only one other known occurrence—in a Portland hospital some years ago. There is no way to know for certain where or when I picked it up.

Getting back to full health has been a yearlong process, with countless doctor visits and therapies. Because God slowed down my body, He gave me the gift of time—a precious gift that allowed this book to be written.

My illness was a life-changing event for our family, many of our friends, and people we don't even know. Shortly after being admitted to the ICU, my son Jon started a blog. Over the course of forty-two days, more than ten thousand unique users from seventy-five countries were praying, monitoring the life-and-death struggle, and watching God's providential healing against all odds. It was a global movement of prayer that only God could have orchestrated; through it we all learned in a new way the amazing power of God to do the miraculous in our day.

The lessons I learned through this difficult time have filled a journal. The front page of the journal sums up those lessons with this entry: "More than ever, I am aware that every day is an undeserved gift from God. That I owe Him my life and that He has graciously granted me additional time to serve Him. I don't deserve it, but that is the nature of grace."

In my first week home after six weeks in the hospital, I asked Mary Ann, "Do you regret that this happened?" She was quiet for some time, and then she said, "No, but I never want to go through it again." Both of us are deeply thankful for what God did and what He has taught us. Hard as it was, we would not trade the experience for anything.

The painful times of life contribute to our legacy through God's gracious redemption of the pain for His eternal purposes. The greatest life and spiritual lessons cannot be learned in any other context.

Take a moment and consider the pain that you have encountered on your journey. Are you willing to thank God for His grace in the pain and ask Him to redeem the pain for your good and His glory? I encourage you to reflect and write down some thoughts about how your pain has shaped your character and your impact on others.

TRANSFORMING FORGIVENESS
INTO LEGACY

Like pain, our ability to forgive those who have wronged us has a direct impact on our legacy. True legacy is not about the success we have accomplished but about the lives we have affected. When we refuse to forgive those who have wronged us, we rob ourselves of the ability to influence them. Moreover, we live in the prison of our own unforgiveness; what we cannot forgive, we are held hostage by.

Gary told me the story of his bitterness with an individual in his church. He was angry and wanted to strike back and hurt the one who he perceived had wronged him. One day Gary realized he could no longer *feel* anything—not for his wife, his kids, or his job. He had no energy, no drive, and no ability to concentrate. He began experiencing serious heart symptoms and fatigue that finally drove him to the hospital, convinced that he was suffering from severe illness.

Indeed he was, but his physical symptoms had no medical explanation. In fact, the doctor said there was nothing wrong and sent him home. But nothing had changed and Gary could barely function. Then one day, sitting in church, Gary pleaded with God to help him.

"It was like God said to me, 'Do you really want to hear what I have to say?'" Gary recalled.

When Gary said yes, God seemed to reply, "Forgive the one you are bitter with and make things right."

In his desperation, Gary said, "Okay, God."

He made an appointment as fast as he could with the person against whom he had harbored bitterness, and the two talked for a long time. Finally, Gary felt the willingness to forgive. And when he did, his debilitating symptoms left—instantly.

I could relate to Gary's struggle. That's because, during one period of my life, I experienced deep hurt because of the mistreatment of others. It was a situation that left me clinically depressed, deeply discouraged, and emotionally wounded

From a human perspective, if anyone did not deserve my forgiveness, it was those who I felt had violated me. But I was left with a dilemma: As long as I held on to the hurt and offense that had been committed, I could not move beyond the pain inflicted on me. But if, on the other hand, I was willing to offer what I thought they did not deserve—my forgiveness—I could move beyond the prison of pain and allow the experience to mold my character. It is a dilemma all of us face when others have hurt us.

Forgiving those individuals from my heart was one of the hardest things I ever did. The pain was severe. But once I took the step, I was on a journey toward freedom, even though it took years to finish. Had I not taken that first step by faith, I would still be imprisoned by bitterness and painful memories. Today, neither has a hold on my life, and I can honestly say that the experience contributed to my growth in numerous ways. God took the pain and redeemed it for His purposes.

When we forgive, we not only obey Jesus' command but we also release the hold those who have wronged us have on our lives. In releasing the bitterness, we give God the opportunity to redeem the pain. When we choose not to forgive, we allow those who wronged us to continue having power over us—and we prevent God from redeeming the pain and turning it into a legacy builder.

Take a moment to think back. Write down the initials of anyone for whom you may harbor feelings of unforgiveness. Are you willing to forgive him or her today so that you can live in freedom and allow God to turn the offense into a positive, constructive part of your life legacy?

TRANSFORMING CHARACTER INTO LEGACY

Meaningful legacy can only be built on character. Peter understood this when he wrote,

> His divine power has given us everything we need for life and godliness through our knowledge of him who called us by his own glory and goodness. Through these he has given us his very great and precious promises, so that through them you may participate in the divine nature and escape the corruption in the world caused by evil desires. (2 Peter 1:3-4)

Through our relationship with Jesus Christ, we allow Him to mold our lives so we actually "participate in the divine nature" of Christ. This involves a commitment to rid our lives of those things that would rob us of legacy—"the corruption in the world caused by evil desires." Peter named eight qualities that directly affect our character and therefore our legacy. He told us to intentionally work on adding these qualities to our lives (see 2 Peter 1:5-8). The eight qualities include:

Faith. Faith involves trusting in Jesus Christ and giving Him the steering wheel of our lives. We understand that life is not about us but about Him, and we can trust Him in all circumstances of life. Faith frees us from anxiety and allows us to focus on living a life pleasing to Him. It is operating from a God-centered, rather than a self-centered, perspective.

Goodness. At the heart of goodness is a way of life that seeks to demonstrate respect, fairness, and compassion to everyone we meet. Goodness takes the focus off ourselves and places it on others. It is a life of generosity rather than selfishness. God was totally "others centered" when He sent His Son to be the sacrifice for our sin. We are invited to join Christ in His work through the goodness and kindness we show others.

Knowledge. Peter was referring to knowledge of God and His Word, which is our ultimate source of instruction and guidance. People of character take that knowledge, accept it as truth, and consciously align their lives to reflect the truth God has given us.

Self-control. Character is impossible without self-control, which is the discipline to say no to wrong and yes to right, to serve others rather than ourselves, and to make life choices that please God. Self-controlled people intentionally harness natural urges that run counter to God's plan for our lives.

Perseverance. Following Christ is a marathon, not a sprint. All of us face disappointments, tough circumstances, illness, and uncertainty. The person of character remains steadfast in his devotion to God and trust in His goodness, even in the darkest moments. Persevering people never give up, and they don't wimp out when life gets rough.

Godliness. This means pursing holiness, purity, and righteousness as a way of life. It means intentionally choosing to follow God, even in areas where our natural bent would be to do otherwise. It is the resolve to follow Christ diligently and wholeheartedly.

Brotherly kindness. Christ followers strive to be loving and generous at all times. They go out of their way to serve others. They care about the marginalized, the poor, the hurting, and the needy.

Love. People of character love God and others. They are "others focused" rather than "self-focused." They forgive, display patience, practice simple acts of kindness, and become the hands, voice, and feet of Jesus to those around them.

Take a moment to review the eight qualities mentioned above, examining your actions and attitudes in each area. Ask God to reveal to you where you can improve in living out His character attributes.

THE BOTTOM LINE

Legacy comes from character, and character comes from intentionally cooperating with Christ and allowing Him to transform our lives in ways that please Him. Those who leave the best legacy are those who have been deliberate and purposeful in allowing God to mold their lives.

God has given us a unique role to play as well as the gifts we need to fulfill that role. He has given us an opportunity to leave a lasting and eternal legacy. What we do with our opportunity is up to us.

Like the stewards in the parable of the talents, each of us has a choice. Our choice will determine the level of regret we may have at the end of our lives and the pleasure our heavenly Father will express for how we invested our time and talents. Will we settle for mediocrity, or will we serve God with heart and soul in a way that ensures a legacy that outlives us? Our answer to this question is one of the most important decisions we will ever make—no matter what our age.

Reflective Prayer

Father, I want to be like the servants in the parable of the talents who were faithful with what You gave them. Like Paul, I want to finish the race well and keep the faith to the end. Like Jesus, I want to complete the work You have given me. Help me pay attention to the areas of life that are critical to leaving an eternal legacy. Thank You for allowing my life to count for eternity. Amen.

For Group Discussion

- As you think about the parable of the talents (see Matthew 25:14-30), what are the "talents" that God has entrusted to you to use on His behalf?
- What potential dangers do you face that would keep you from maximizing your eternal legacy?
- Are there changes you need to make in order to finish well, minimize regrets, and maximize your legacy?
- Think back on our discussion from the last chapter about the way God has wired you and gifted you. In what ways can you utilize your unique strengths and talents to leave a lasting legacy?

Chapter 4

WHAT REALLY MATTERS?

ESTABLISHING CLEAR PRIORITIES

Teach us to number our days aright, that we may gain a heart of wisdom.

— PSALM 90:12

Think for a moment about all the obligations you have in the coming four weeks.

Are you tired yet?

Whatever happened to those long, leisurely dinners when the whole family came together? Or the traditional Sunday lunch at Grandma's house served with the finest set of dishes and silverware? Or summer evenings on the front porch with a pitcher of lemonade?

These days, life moves at warp speed with more sporting events than we can handle, more obligations than we desire, and more demands and deadlines than we can keep up with. Not even our numerous time-saving devices help us find adequate margin in our lives. The options and obligations that bombard us seem to multiply faster than cockroaches.

In the previous chapters we have examined the importance of living at the intersection of God's call and our willingness to embrace that call.

Perhaps you have found yourself saying, "I don't have time for that." How often we put off what is truly meaningful to attend to what is merely urgent. We squander the chance to build a lasting legacy by always attending to the demands of the moment.

The one resource we can never get back, the one resource more precious than any other, is time. Prioritizing our lives so that we use the gift of time effectively is one of the most important endeavors we'll ever undertake. Ironically, we are often too busy to slow down long enough to think through this issue. Busyness robs us of the time needed to decide how we ought to spend our time!

In our hustle and bustle, many of us are running on empty — physically, emotionally, and spiritually. We accept this as normal, but I suggest there is a better way to handle our jam-packed, stress-filled lives. The solution is to carefully consider and answer the question, "What *really* matters?"

I hope you have been challenged and encouraged by the first three questions dealing with your purpose, the way you're wired, and the legacy you want to leave. In a real way, this fourth question empowers and enables the first three — that is, unless we are strategic in our use of time, we will not fulfill the promise behind those earlier questions. It all has to do with priorities.

Moses understood this truth. He wrote the psalm that began this chapter. Moses understood that there is an equation between the time God grants us and the wisdom it takes to use that time wisely. Time cannot be taken for granted, and wise living takes into account those things that make the heart of God glad. Wise people recognize the brevity of life and the priorities God has for them.

Contrast that view with how most people live — with little thought for how they use their time, usually allowing obligations, crises, the expectations of others, and the "stuff of life" to dictate their schedules. Such "accidental living" is characterized by these habits:

- Living by the moment
- Harried and hurried

- Little advance planning
- Busy but without well-defined priorities
- Enslaved by the expectations of others
- Flying through life on autopilot

It is difficult to reconcile those habits with Moses' admonition to "number our days" and "gain a heart of wisdom." Moses pointed to a life characterized by an entirely different set of habits, a life we can call "intentional living":

- Determine time use by life priorities
- Give significant thought and planning to the use of time
- Consult with our Lord on commitments, obligations, and priorities
- Say no to some *good* things in order to say yes to *better* things
- Build in time for the most important priorities before allocating time for discretionary options

I can guess which of the above lists you find most appealing. We all do! We will leave behind the accidental life and enjoy the intentional life only when we establish clear priorities and pay close attention to our use of time.

THE MOST VALUABLE RESOURCE

Time is more precious than money. After all, money comes and goes, but time just goes. Many of us would give up some of our money for more time. One of my staff members last year asked if he could negotiate an extra week off each year in lieu of a raise. If there is one commodity I personally wish I had more of, it would be time.

Our approach to finances can be a model for how we approach our time. In our household — and maybe yours, too — we do a lot of thinking about how we use our financial resources. They are finite, and at any given time we must make choices about how we will use our available dollars and prioritize our list of needs and wants.

Most people work with some kind of a budget (or should) where we allocate certain percentages of our dollars toward specific obligations. We start with the nonnegotiable costs, such as our mortgage and utilities, and after the essentials we have discretionary dollars we can use for our wish list. Whether we have relatively little or relatively much, we must think carefully about our financial resources and prioritize their use.

What if we approached our time the same way? We have a portfolio of time: daily, weekly, monthly, and annually. What would happen if we were to scrutinize just as carefully the use of our time, how we allocate our hours, and where they will be spent? After all, the decisions we make based on our priorities will determine how well we live, the legacy we leave, and whether we accomplish the work God uniquely designed us for.

Those who take their finances for granted and do not plan or prioritize find themselves in a financial ditch. In the same way, if we take our time for granted and are not discriminating in how we use it, we will one day wish we had made better choices. We need God's wisdom regarding our schedules. What I want to help you think through is a way of prioritizing and allocating your portfolio of time to provide increased freedom, more joy, less stress, and greater life results.

DEVELOPING A THEOLOGY OF TIME

Our challenge as Christ followers is to recognize that there are competing philosophies about how we view time, resources, and gifting. The prevailing philosophy of our culture is that these are "mine" and I can do whatever I choose with them. It is a self-centered attitude that views resources as our own—to be used for our pleasure, leisure, and advancement. We sometimes think that when we throw a bit of our time or energy God's way, we have done Him a favor.

This philosophy is directly at odds with how Scripture sees time, financial resources, and talents. Scripture starts with the proposition that these are gifts from God and that we are merely stewards of them. As Jesus taught in the parable of the talents, we will be held accountable for how we use the resources God has given us to use on His behalf. Everything we have is owned by the Father and entrusted to us to use wisely and generously. This is a God-centered view of our resources.

To live an accidental life is to treat our God-given resources with carelessness and recklessness. To choose a self-centered view is to deny His ownership and to live in disobedience. Interestingly, Scripture defines sin as going our own way or doing our own thing without regard to our Creator (see Isaiah 53:6). And that's how most of us tend to view our use of time.

The goal for Christ followers is to approach all of life with utmost reverence and respect for the Creator's gifts. This is what Paul was getting at when he said,

> Therefore, I urge you, brothers, in view of God's mercy, to offer your bodies as living sacrifices, holy and pleasing to God—this is your spiritual act of worship. Do not conform any longer to the pattern of this world, but be transformed by the renewing of your mind. (Romans 12:1-2)

This includes our use of time, which we must grapple with all of our lives.

Some years ago I was approached by a firm that asked me to join them and head up their consulting for evangelical ministry organizations. The annual salary they offered was nearly triple my salary at the time. From a human point of view, it was enticing. But because I understand what God has called me to do, it wasn't even an option. I would not be happy doing something that was not in the center of God's will for my life. We all make choices and those choices have consequences.

PUTTING FIRST THINGS FIRST

Because time is a finite commodity and we are stewards of God-given resources, we must make difficult choices that affect our lives. I have a close friend who taught me to fly-fish, a hobby I have come to love. This friend does not fly-fish when he is home in Wisconsin but only when he is on vacation. When I asked him why he didn't fish the streams close to home, he said, "I know myself and how easily I can use my time for my own pleasure. I would rather go several times a year and concentrate on fly-fishing so that when I am home, I can concentrate on other things."

It may seem like a small thing, but he is doing what all of us must do — make choices about time usage that reflect our priorities. If we approach our time from a me perspective, we simply choose whatever pleases us the most. If we choose how we use our time from a God perspective, we ensure that we have life in balance with His leading.

Take the following common priorities: marriage, family, close friends, occupation, service commitments, recreation, devotional time, personal development, elderly parents, church involvement. Whatever mix you have, depending on your life stage and circumstances, these are the kinds of priorities that need to be balanced. Life is a series of choices, each of which tests our wisdom, convictions, and desire to please our Lord. God asks us to make those choices in ways that are consistent with our service to Him and His kingdom, with the wisdom that comes from prayerful consideration.

Spend a few moments listing the key priorities that take up your time and then ranking them in order of relative importance. Once you've done that, consider two questions: How are you doing in prioritizing these in real life? Are you satisfied that you have the right priorities?

THE POWER OF NO

The truth that we have finite time forces us to choose between many opportunities, options, and obligations. We must say yes to the most important, maybe to other possibilities, and a gracious no to those things that don't align with our priorities. We cannot do everything and do it well. What's more, we cannot do everything and keep our sanity! Living a life of focus involves utilizing the power of the word *no*.

It is amazing how many people "have a wonderful plan for your life."

They may be family members, supervisors, parents, volunteer coordinators, or church staff. Lots of people are pretty sure how you should be spending your time and energy. That's why some of the most liberating words are "Thanks for the opportunity, but I really can't accept at this time." Or simply "No, thank you."

Here is the reality: We cannot meet every expectation and please every person who presents an opportunity. But God provides us with ample time to do what He has called us to do. If we are clear about God's priorities for our lives, we can sift through the options and determine, on the basis of those priorities, what we will and won't do. In my job I have opportunities to do many things I enjoy. They are good things and often fun things. But if I am going to be fruitful in fulfilling my top priorities, I need to decline some things—not because they aren't important for someone, but because they are not priorities for me.

This principle also applies to my personal time and ministry focus. I need to determine where to invest time in order to live at the intersection of God's call and my willingness to accept that call. One of the assignments God has given me is to write books that will help ministries, churches, and Christ followers become all they can be. Since I have a full-time job, I have to carve out personal time in order to achieve this goal. I need to decline some opportunities in order to accomplish what is, for me, a higher priority.

Busyness is the enemy of fruitfulness. Think about this: Everyone is busy, but not everyone is equally fruitful. Busyness does not equal results! Those who see the most significant ministry or work results do fewer things and focus on the most important things—according to their unique priorities. I have found it helpful to discuss any opportunities with Mary Ann (or someone else who knows me well) before saying yes. Sometimes other people can be more objective than me when it comes to evaluating requests.

Ironically, doing less often helps us accomplish more. A balanced schedule gives us time to think and plan. It allows us to do things well rather than second rate. Even Jesus realized that He should say no to some opportunities. In Mark 1, we read that Jesus was in Capernaum, where he healed Simon's mother-in-law and "many who had various diseases. He also drove out many demons" (verse 34). Early the next morning Jesus went to a quiet place to pray. When Simon and his companions found Jesus, they said, "Everyone is looking for you!" (verse 37). They wanted Jesus to return to town and continue what He had been doing the previous day.

Jesus' response is surprising. Rather than doing what the disciples expected, He replied, "Let us go somewhere else—to the nearby villages—so I can preach there also" (verse 38). In other words, He said no to the needs and expectations because He had more important missional things to do.

Jesus understood the power of saying no because He distinguished between things that were good and things that were critical for His ministry. He determined what He needed to do rather than allowing others to define those things for Him. It should not be lost on us that Jesus said no to the disciples' request after He had spent time with His Father. Jesus was in the habit of taking time to refresh His intimacy with the Father and pray about decisions.

Think through your current schedule and evaluate whether there are obligations you need to relinquish in order to focus on the most important things God has called you to. Write down areas where you may need to modify your schedule in order to be more intentional and fruitful in your areas of priority.

PEOPLE ARE A PRIORITY

When reading the Gospels we cannot help but notice how much time Jesus spent with people. He was almost always with people; of course, that is why He came to earth in the first place. Many of those He spent time with were the sick, the poor, the outcasts, the sinful, and those shunned by the religious establishment.

I love it! Jesus was a friend to those who truly needed a friend, needed grace, and were receptive to good news. Time with the marginalized was a priority for Christ. He willingly talked with skeptics, tax collectors, prostitutes, and adulterers. No one was out of bounds.

Followers of Christ—like Christ Himself—make people a priority. And that takes time. If we see people as deeply loved by God and precious to Him, we'll be amazed at how many opportunities we have to interact with neighbors, flight attendants, restaurant servers, doctors and nurses, grocery store clerks, and teachers at our kids' schools. On and on it goes. You will never regret spending time with:

- Your spouse
- Your children and your grandchildren
- Lifelong friends who share the journey with you
- Your neighbors
- People in your small group
- Those you mentor (formally or informally)
- Those who mentor or influence you
- The hurting, marginalized, or lonely
- Those you can help with small acts of kindness
- The people who come across your path in the normal course of life

The common denominator here is people. Much of our time investment is with people, and that investment has eternal value. There are only three things that cross the line from earthly time to eternity: (1) our spiritual maturity, which comes in large part from our time with our heavenly Father; (2) the lives we have influenced, which comes in large part from our time with others; and (3) the financial investments we have made that brought people to Christ or helped them grow in Him. It is easy for those who are task-driven to think we don't have time to slow down for people. The investments we make in people are the ones that will pay eternal dividends.

MARGIN MATTERS

It's true that much of our influence and ministry revolves around relationships. It's also true that people and their needs usually don't fit into neat, tidy time slots. Demands and difficulties seem to come at the most inconvenient times. Life happens, and when it does, we need the margin—time and energy reserves—to respond effectively.

When I went into the hospital on December 4, 2007, two of our closest friends dropped nearly everything and spent most of the next forty-two days ministering to my family as I hovered between life and death. Other close friends and my large extended family did the same. Two of my key prayer partners flew to St. Paul to spend days interceding for me and the family.

Mary Ann, Steven, and Jon would not have made it through that time without their support. I was amazed and humbled by the many people who visited, wrote, or ministered to our family during those very dark days. We discover who loves us when a crisis occurs!

For people who live at a fast pace, it's not easy to drop everything and be there for someone in need. But the ability to stop, interact, and help is huge in terms of the impact we will have. A willingness to readjust schedules to be with someone during a tough time, make an encouraging phone call, or write a thoughtful note—those things mean more than we will ever know. I am convinced that our personal interaction with those around us is perhaps the most powerful ministry we will ever have.

I have learned over the years that I need to cut back on the pace I maintain—for my health and effectiveness and for the sake of those I come into contact with. If all we are to others is a passing acquaintance, too busy to connect, we will never be seen as someone who cares. I have met people who breeze in and out and give the impression they are too busy with "more important" things to interact in an authentic way. I am left with a sad feeling when I see them. Whatever interest they show seems disingenuous.

In the course of a week, we meet many people who are hurting, some we don't even know. They respond with gratefulness when someone takes the time to ask them about their day, offer a word of encouragement, or say a brief prayer on their behalf. Several years ago I attended a conference in Lisbon, Portugal. Some of us had access to the business lounge and developed relationships with a few of the young people who worked there. Near the end of the conference, friends of mine thought a particular young lady seemed sad. They asked if they could pray for her, and she said yes. They prayed, not knowing her situation. When they were done, tears were running down her cheeks, and she said, "No one has ever prayed for me before!" She was deeply moved, all because a few people cared about her as a person and took the time to discern that she had a need.

The more we pack our schedules, the less time we have for the people around us whom God has placed in our path. Margin matters — it allows us to respond when needs arise.

CONNECT THE COMPASS TO THE CLOCK

The key to translating our commitments into action is to connect our priorities with our calendars. Another way to say it is, we need to connect the compass to the clock. Our priorities — those things that are most important in our lives — keep us moving in the right direction. When we synchronize those priorities with how we use our time (and calendars), we connect the compass with the clock.

Most of us use some kind of scheduling plan. Because my life is filled with meetings, phone appointments, and travel, I use an electronic calendar that syncs with my phone. Before a new month begins, I look at my priorities and my calendar and start blocking out time for important obligations; that way my priorities drive my schedule rather than the demands of daily life. I encourage you to do the same. If you are married and have a weekly date with your spouse, put it on the calendar. If, like us, you have a commitment to a set of lifelong friends, make sure time with them is on your calendar.

After you finish updating your monthly schedule, you should be able to compare your list of priorities with your calendar and see tangible evidence of your priorities. I actually use color options on my electronic calendar to note my highest priorities so that I have a visual picture of how the most significant things in my life translate into time commitments. This exercise is the most critical thing I do to ensure that I am living out the priorities God has for me. If at the end of my monthly planning I realize I have a jam-packed schedule lacking margin, I can go back and try to take out the least important pieces to create breathing space.

Doing this also gives me flexibility when someone asks me to do something on short notice. I can say, "You know, it won't work this month, but we could talk about a later date." It also forces me to plan ahead—a sign of an intentional life—rather than flying by the seat of my pants. Because I have left margin in my schedule, I still have the flexibility to add people time as I choose.

ACTIVITY VERSUS RESULTS

The reason we make the effort to carefully consider our schedule is that it allows us to see greater results from our lives. Remember, activity does not equal results. Fruitfulness comes when we plan ahead so that our priorities get the attention they deserve and are carefully planned into our week and month. The most effective individuals are those who spend significant time thinking about their schedules, determining in advance what they will and will not do.

Because we are planning ahead, when new opportunities, requests, or possibilities surface, we simply keep a running list of those items. As we think about our next month, we can determine whether those opportunities fit our schedule. After consideration, we may find ourselves saying, "That one does not fit my priorities right now." Or "This is something I ought to do." Or perhaps "I'm going to keep thinking about that."

I suggest setting aside anywhere from two to four hours each month to plan for the following month. This is your monthly personal retreat—either by yourself or with your spouse—when you can think through the priorities of your life, evaluate the past month, and carefully plan the next month. During that time, ponder these questions:

- How did last month go? Was I successful in meeting the priorities I believe God has for me? If I could do it over, what would I do differently?

- If there is one thing that is absolutely critical to do this coming month, what would it be?
- Does my schedule for next month reflect my priorities?
- Has God been speaking to me about anything in my life or schedule that I need to take into consideration?
- Am I happy with the balance and margin in my schedule?

I take this a step further by taking time out toward the end of each year to evaluate the prior year in light of my priorities and prayerfully consider what God wants me to accomplish in the coming year. This is a combination of thinking, planning, praying, and listening to God. My goal is that every year I become more fruitful because I live a little smarter and focus a little better. I am encouraged every year when I can look back and see that I have progressed in some way.

Some of us are natural planners while others are not. If you are not, I challenge you to try this for at least three months. I am confident that the longer you do it, the easier it will become and the more satisfied you will be with how you are managing your time. Once you get the hang of it, you'll find yourself in a natural routine of thinking ahead, keeping your priorities in mind, and living with greater intentionality.

You may be thinking, *Wow, I don't want to be that rigid and disciplined in my schedule or planning.* I understand. Let me suggest that the reason we do this is not to be rigid and disciplined but because we want our lives to reap the greatest possible fruit. Our planning is simply a way to get to where we want to be. With unlimited options but limited time, we need a tool like this to ensure that we keep our lives in alignment with our priorities.

In John 15, Jesus said, "I am the vine; you are the branches. If a man remains in me and I in him, he will bear much fruit" (verse 5). Deciding to be intentional about our use of time is really a decision to live in a way that will bear the most fruit possible. That fruit is directly connected with how God has gifted us and the unique work He has designed for us.

TIME ENOUGH TO FULFILL YOUR CALLING

In Psalm 139:16, David wrote, "All the days ordained for me were written in your book before one of them came to be." Just as God provides ample skills and strengths to accomplish the mission He gives us, He also provides adequate time. Our challenge is to use that time well.

My work takes me to places of the world that are not always safe. I sometimes must deal with airlines that have difficulty keeping their planes in the sky, traffic laws that are only vague suggestions, and poor medical care should one need it (reused needles, anyone?). I have had my share of close calls over the years. Two hotels I've stayed in have been targets of terrorist attacks (fortunately, not when I was there).

A lesson I learned from my hospital stay from December 4, 2007, to January 14, 2008, is that God is absolutely sovereign over my life. By all human reasoning, I should not be here today. In a very dark moment, one of my wonderful doctors stood at the foot of my bed and mumbled, "We really need outside intervention here." He was right.

I count January 14, 2008, the day I left the hospital after forty-two days, as my second birthday. God granted me additional time because in His sovereign plan the "days ordained for me" were not complete. I realized sometime later that I had lost all fear of death (the vague fear that lurks in the back of our minds), knowing that I will not leave this earth until I have completed the days He has granted me. In the meantime, I want to make every day count!

THE BOTTOM LINE

God made us to be in relationship with Him and to join Him in His work. God wants us to influence our corner of the world so that His will is done on earth as it is done in heaven. We are stewards of the gifts He has bestowed upon us, and through our active involvement in His work we will see eternal results.

We should care about clarifying our priorities and tying our time commitments to those priorities because this allows us to fulfill God's unique role for our lives and leave a meaningful legacy. Our time is a precious investment that, once used, we can never get back. Treat it as the valuable commodity that it is.

REFLECTIVE PRAYER

Father, teach me to number my days so that I will use the time You have given me in ways that will count for eternity. Grant me wisdom to know those things I should put first and those areas I should reorient in my life. Thank You for inviting me to join You in Your work. Amen.

For Group Discussion

- Share with one another the highest priorities in your lives.
- What are the challenges you face in fulfilling the true priorities of life, and what strategies do you use to overcome those challenges?
- Are there areas of life that you are rethinking as a result of answering this chapter's key question?
- How do you use the power of no to stay engaged with the most important things, and how has it worked for you?

Chapter 5

WHAT IS MY PLAN?

DETERMINING EFFECTIVE WAYS TO GROW AND DEVELOP

Do you not know that in a race all the runners run, but only one gets the prize? Run in such a way as to get the prize. Everyone who competes in the games goes into strict training. They do it to get a crown that will not last; but we do it to get a crown that will last forever.

— 1 CORINTHIANS 9:24-25

Many Olympics have a defining moment or a particular athlete who seems to overshadow the games. In the Beijing 2008 Olympics, it was Michael Phelps, who walked away with eight gold medals, winning the gold in each of the events he entered and setting new world records in seven of those races.

The unforgettable moment was Phelps's seventh race — the one-hundred–meter butterfly — in which he was lagging behind Serbia's Milorad Čavić. Twenty feet from the end of the race, Phelps gathered his strength and lunged for the wall, beating Čavić by *one one-hundredth* of a second. The replays of that last split second were shown over and over. While Čavić glided to his finish, Phelps made a final lunge that proved to be the difference.

Behind Phelps's remarkable showing were years of disciplined training from the age of seven. His victories were the culmination of countless hours of training and an extraordinary regimen to prepare his body and mind. The discipline needed to make it to the Olympics is massive, as is the commitment to become all that we can be.

Like Michael Phelps, we also are in a race. Our race is not for a moment of glory and a gold medal but a lifetime of service to the Lord of the universe, an eternal legacy that comes from living at the intersection of God's call and our response to that call. We strive for, as Paul said, "a crown that will last forever." As is true for those who compete in the Olympics, finishing well and accomplishing God's will for our lives does not happen without a plan and the discipline to keep growing.

I am inspired by the apostle Paul, who never stopped pushing himself, never stopped learning, never retired from ministry, and always had vision for the future. Writing to the Corinthians, he said,

> Do you not know that in a race all the runners run, but only one gets the prize? Run in such a way as to get the prize. Everyone who competes in the games goes into strict training. They do it to get a crown that will not last; but we do it to get a crown that will last forever. Therefore I do not run like a man running aimlessly; I do not fight like a man beating the air. No, I beat my body and make it my slave so that after I have preached to others, I myself will not be disqualified for the prize. (1 Corinthians 9:24-27)

Painting a picture of one obsessed with continuing to grow, Paul described how he used the gifts God had given him to fulfill the work God had for him. He compared his commitment to that of an athlete who "goes into strict training." The day we stop growing is the day we start leaving opportunity on the table. The race is not over until the contestant lunges toward victory, like Michael Phelps, and crosses the finish line. Our race is not over until we cross the line from time to eternity.

God created us to be in relationship with Him and to join Him in His work. He gives us gifts and strengths, empowered by His Spirit, to fulfill our unique roles. Our path to legacy involves continual, intentional growth—in our gifts, spiritual maturity, relationships, and emotional lives. We may retire from our occupation, but there is no retirement from ministry, influence, and legacy building.

It saddens me to see people retire from active ministry like they do from their jobs, thinking that a life of leisure will satisfy their souls. That is a colossal waste of what could be the most significant years of influence. My hundred-year-old friend, Naomi, still has significant influence because she has chosen to stay in the game, to keep growing, and to use her strengths for God. She tells me that the past twenty years have been the most fulfilling of her life and that she has grown more during those years than during the rest of her life combined. Like Naomi, the best thing you and I can do is intentionally hone our God-given strengths so that as the years pass, our influence will grow instead of wane.

IT TAKES A PLAN

In the passage from 1 Corinthians 9, Paul made two interesting comments. He said, "I do not run like a man running aimlessly; I do not fight like a man beating the air." His point was that there is a race to be run for Christ, and Paul was intentional about how he ran, how he matured as a believer, and how he went about his ministry. There was nothing accidental about how Paul lived his life. He was strategic. We know he prayerfully thought through his priorities and his travels. He intentionally discipled and mentored individuals who had promise. He lived a life of intentional discipline designed to maximize his influence for Christ.

Why do people hire executive or personal coaches? Because they want to maximize their potential, stay sharp, keep getting better at what they do, and continue to develop. It is a smart thing to do and a biblical thing to do, but it takes a plan.

There is no magic bullet for continuing to grow, learn, and develop. Each of us has a way of learning that works for us, so personal development needs to fit our particular personality, temperament, and learning style. That being said, I believe there are some key practices that directly relate to maximizing our growth, our potential, and therefore our legacy.

PEOPLE WE KNOW

If you surround yourself with people who are wiser than you, some of their wisdom will rub off. The most influential people I know are deeply intentional about their relationships. They pursue relationships with individuals they respect and can learn from.

God has blessed Mary Ann and me with some of the most outstanding friends we could possibly hope for. Each of them has influenced us in specific ways, including our faith, marriage, leadership, relationship skills, and on and on. This rich mosaic of quality friends has left an indelible mark on our lives. We have a saying: "friends for life." We intentionally pursue relationships with people who want to share the journey with us, and we are intentional in keeping those relationships current.

If you invest in healthy relationships with people who are passionate about living out their lives for maximum impact, you will be deeply influenced by them. The advice most of us got as kids is true: We become like the friends we keep. We have many friendships, but we nurture our key friendships, which are more precious than all the gold in the world. These key relationships can speak into our lives and tell us truth, and we know that we can trust them explicitly. These are the friends who encourage us, help us, and share our joys and burdens.

All of us have friends, but not all of us cultivate deep friendships that have the power to help us grow and become all God made us to be. Key friendships are an investment to be nurtured. For Mary Ann and me, our "friends for life" are high on the list of priorities and take precedence in our schedule.

While not all of our close relationships will be with fellow Christ followers, it is imperative that a core of them share our beliefs and values. Paul told us in several places to "encourage one another" and "spur one another on to good works." Only those who have such passion and commitment can help us do that.

Our friends matter if we are going to keep growing and stay on the cutting edge of life and ministry. Choose your friends carefully and nurture them consistently. Each of my friends is a faithful mentor in some area of life, not formally but informally. They have helped me grow and develop. And it's a joy to be with them and to experience life together.

Do you have "friends for life" who challenge you, influence you, and gently push you to be all that you can be as a Christ follower? In your journal or a notebook, name them and take a moment to thank God for the gift of their friendship.

BOOKS WE READ

Books — really good books — are like relationships. They mold us, inspire us, and cause us to think deeply. The issue is not how many books we read but the quality of the books we read. C. S. Lewis is a close friend of mine; I have enjoyed his company while spending a great deal of time with him through his writings. Another hero of mine is Winston Churchill, with whom I have also spent many hours (minus the cigar smoke).

Choose your books with care. As it says on the T-shirt book lovers wear: *So many books, so little time.* Read those that will challenge your thinking rather than simply entertain you or confirm what you already know. Shallow thinking is one of the sins of our time. As I get older, I spend less time with popular light books and far more time with those that grip my heart and prompt me to think deeply. Read with concentration and engagement, allowing the writer to stimulate your thoughts. Read classics as well as current works. Many of the sharpest thinkers are long gone, but you can meet them in their writing.

Some people are not naturally readers. That is okay. A number of the smartest people I know are not. But all of us need the wisdom of others. If reading is not in your sweet spot, consider listening to books on CD or on your iPod while driving or jogging. It takes intentionality and discipline to find time to be challenged by others through their writing.

The prevalence of the Internet and the ubiquitous nature of television can rob us of time better spent. I enjoy both! However, with the plethora of options we have for spending our leisure time, we need to make choices, even small ones, about our time. Some choices are more productive than others.

What were the last five significant books you read? Do you have a reading plan that is designed to stretch you and cause you to think deeply? Make a list of your most meaningful books and recommend them to your friends and family members.

EXPERIENCES WE CHOOSE

Experiences can change our lives, our perspectives, and our understanding. I remember inviting Jot and Marietta to travel to China with a small group I was leading. Jot later told me, "I thought, *Why would I want to go to China?*" But they came along and have since made many trips back, leading service teams and taking part in China ministry.

While we all love good experiences, the trick is to choose some that will stretch us and take us out of our comfort zones. Whenever I travel internationally, I ask to be brought to the poorest area of town. I know that 54 percent of our world lives on three dollars a day or less. I want a reality check as well as to see what God is doing in amazingly tough circumstances. You cannot make many of those trips without coming away changed and more deeply committed to ministries that help the less fortunate.

I vividly remember a trip to a Manila slum, home to hundreds of thousands of destitute men, women, and children. I visited with a family who lived in a shack on stilts along a canal of sludge and sewage. One of the daughters was fifteen years old and spoke fluent English. I asked her what she wanted to be when she was an adult. She said, "A doctor — to help people like this." As I stood there in the mud, I wondered what the probability was that this young lady would fulfill her dream. She was, after all, from a family scraping by on a dollar a day by making cheap plastic shoes.

Experiences like this in the crowded cities of our world have profoundly influenced my life and my commitment to holistic ministry

—ministry that shares the good news of Jesus while helping the needy in tangible ways. That is the heart of Jesus; it has always been the heart of God (see Isaiah 58); and it should be our heart too.

I recall a ministry trip our church took to train teachers in rural Yunnan Province in China. When we arrived at the school, we checked out the dorms (with prickly, smelly horsehair mattresses), the toilets (holes in the floor and no plumbing), the food (pretty bad), the bugs (really big), and the air-conditioning (open windows, mosquitoes, and hot nights). Several team members were ready to turn around and go right back home! Yet at the end of the ten-day training period, no one wanted to leave. The amazing friendships they had formed overshadowed their minus-two-star accommodations.

Most life-changing experiences we participate in involve ministry that is outside of our cozy cocoons. This requires a willingness to risk leaving our places of security and convenience. I have yet to meet anyone who has stepped out of his comfort zone to minister to the poor and disadvantaged without his own life becoming radically changed.

What are the three most significant experiences of your life that caused you to stretch and grow? Have you had any in the past twelve months?

DEFINING MOMENTS WE EXPERIENCE

Life grants us many lessons that we did not intend to learn, and they are often the most valuable lessons we receive. All those who have reached the fifty-year mark can look back over unforeseen events, circumstances, and heartaches that came our way and molded us as nothing else could: illness, bankruptcy, death of loved ones, people who betrayed us, failures, divorce, infidelity, job loss, depression, or children who made poor choices. These are defining moments in our lives, and depending on how we respond to them, they bring either growth or bitterness.

My first real defining moment came in my late twenties when I resigned from the church that I had pastored for three and a half years. The details are not important, but it was a crushing blow. I felt like a failure; my dreams were crushed; and I was tired, depressed, and heartbroken. I did not understand why God had allowed it to happen, and I watched with sorrow as the church I had given my life to and the people I loved split apart after I left.

Mary Ann and I packed our belongings and left for Minnesota, nearly broke, wondering what we would do next. We knew I was not ready to serve as a pastor again until my heart had healed. Eventually, I got a job selling furniture for a friend I had worked for eight years earlier while in college.

The soul-searching in the aftermath of my perceived failure led me on a quest to understand the grace of God. I realized that there was nothing I could do to make God love me any more or any less. I came to see that who I was as a child of God was more important than any job or ministry I could have. I learned what heartbreak felt like and gained insight into the heartache of others. God taught me that success does not mean an absence of failure but learning from failure and being faithful to His calling.

Defining moments of life can be opportunities to grow in ways that we would not otherwise grow, or they can be moments in which we let our lives slip into sadness, allowing the dreams God has given us to evaporate. Sometimes, like in my example, God allows our dreams to be crushed so that we embrace His larger and grander purposes for our lives. The choices we make in response to life's defining moments make all the difference in the world.

What are the defining moments you have experienced in your life, and what did they teach you?

MINISTRY WE UNDERTAKE

Using our gifts in ministry will always help us grow and stay fresh. But doing so can be scary and intimidating as well. Ministry changes us because we are joining God in His work. And when we join Him in His work, nothing stays the same.

Think back to what you have learned about your sweet spot and the kind of work that God has uniquely called you to do. The more we find opportunity to engage in ways He has gifted us, the better we become at it. We grow when we use our gifts, and we stagnate when we don't. This is no different than in our professional lives. The more experience we have at what we do, the better we become at it.

Mary Ann recently received a call from one of her former high school students, a girl she had helped when she became pregnant in ninth grade. Now a senior, she was living with her boyfriend, who was abusing her; she had a two-year-old daughter; and her dad had come to live with them to try to protect her. None of the three was employed. Talk about a messy situation.

Mary Ann rounded up help, called the police to meet her at the apartment, found a place for the dad to live and another place for the young mother and her daughter to live, and then networked to find the dad a job. The gal she rescued was too accustomed to a life of chaos to live in the order she found in her new home, and seven months later she ended up with a different abusive boyfriend. The dad has had his challenges as well, but it looks like he is getting his life together and dealing with the issues that have caused him difficulty in the past.

I love watching Mary Ann pull something like this off. Ministry is often messy, but she is in her sweet spot. In the middle of messes, God changes lives. People become whole and learn to trust Him when things don't go as planned.

When we use our ministry gifts and dive into scary, new, or chaotic situations, we see God work. That experience gives us the faith to take another step, and then another. We have to get over the mind-set that we're not qualified because we're not trained. We have been equipped — not by a seminary or Bible school, but by the God of the universe who has written a job description for each of us. What He wants us to do is take the risk, dive in, and get our hands dirty doing whatever it is He has called and wired us to do.

You cannot stay engaged in real ministry with real people in real situations and not experience growth and change. Every time we take a step of faith and join God in His work, we deepen our own faith and are willing to take an even greater step of faith in the future.

Are you currently engaged in ministry that challenges you and forces you to rely on God's power? What is the most satisfying outreach you were ever involved in? How did it change you?

RISKS WE TAKE

On a regular basis, God calls us, as He called Peter, to step out of our safe, familiar boats and follow Him in some endeavor that requires our total trust. My friend Mark was a successful stockbroker and investment adviser when God called him to start a church in Rockford, Illinois. Mark had no seminary degree and he already had a well-paying job, but he also had a deep passion for those who didn't know Christ.

After exploring many alternatives, Mark and Sherri, along with another couple named Doug and Cindy, decided to start a church in the space they had—their living room. Doug would lead worship, Mark and Sherri would provide the vision and direction, and preaching would be done by video from another church that had a great preaching library.

Guess what people said? "It won't work." "That's not how you do church!" "You need a traditional preaching/leading pastor." But they felt called, so they took the risk. After a few services, the living room became too cramped with people. They purchased a restaurant and conference center and focused on transformational teaching, small groups, and great kids' ministries . . . and the church kept growing.

When they hit the four-thousand mark, they knew they had to find a bigger place. Instead of doing what most churches do—purchase land on the outskirts of town to build on—they bought an old, rundown shopping mall in the center of Rockford. What? A church in a mall?

They were able to get their ministry space for about half of what it would have cost to build, and the businesses that remained in the mall paid most of the mortgage for the church. They also had space to develop on-site ministries for the needy. Being in the center of Rockford gave them accessibility to all of the socioeconomic groups that make up the city.

The risks paid off. The church just celebrated its ten-year anniversary. They have more than seven thousand people and a remote campus in

Madison, Wisconsin. More than two thousand new believers have been baptized in the past decade. On top of that, numerous other churches have studied what Heartland Community Church has done and are emulating its model.

It is always worth taking the risk when it is clear that God is in it. Risk forces us to trust God in ways we have not had to trust Him before. Ironically, our comfort zones are not really conducive to growth. It is in the push-the-envelope zone where we see the most progress.

When we step out to try something God has placed on our hearts, it always feels like a risk. It is not unusual for those around us to ask, "What in the world are you doing?" Sometimes they say, "You're nuts."

God loves it when we take a risk for Him. We may look at the task and say, "I'm not qualified." Or "I can't pull that off." The fact is, we are all unqualified apart from the power He gives us through His Spirit. Christ has given us gifts, and He has given us the power of His Holy Spirit. That is why we can have confidence when we step out of the boat, knowing that God is the one holding us up and leading us on.

What is the largest risk you have ever taken? Is God quietly asking you to take a risk today? If so, how might He be asking you to get out of your familiar boat?

QUESTIONS WE ASK

We grow when we choose to be inquisitive. I enjoy spending time with my friend Ken because he asks tons of questions—about everything. It does not matter if he is meeting with a young person or someone like himself who runs a large corporation. He is always asking, listening, learning.

It is amazing what we can learn from asking questions of the people who come across our path: clerks, neighbors, co-workers, the guy or gal sitting beside you on the flight. As we interact with people around us, we add their information, worldview, and expertise to our own. Besides, people love to be asked about things they know; it honors them and gives them a chance to share their knowledge and experience.

I enjoy asking questions of my sons and other young people. Their views on life, politics, society, and priorities challenge me and help me think from a different perspective. I find the same thing when I engage folks from walks of life that are very different from mine. A by-product of asking questions is that it is an entrée into wonderful conversations that may give us a chance to talk about important matters of life and faith. When we engage others first, they open up and often start to engage us in return.

Asking questions is an art that can be learned. Being an introvert by nature, I have learned to engage people whenever possible rather than opting for my own thoughts. The simple question "What do you think about . . . ?" can open a great conversation, give you a glimpse of a different perspective, and help you learn something new.

OBEDIENCE WE PURSUE

Nothing will cause us to grow, develop, and stretch like a commitment to be a fully devoted follower of Christ. Many have a negotiated commitment. They follow God when it is easy and convenient, but they fudge when things become inconvenient. I believe this is why studies show that there is little difference in lifestyle between those who claim to be Christ followers and the rest of society.

Nonnegotiated commitment means we align our lives with Jesus and Scripture through the empowerment of His Spirit. Every time we take a new step of obedience, we change and grow closer to what God wants us to be. The New Testament is explicit that there are things we are to "put off" and other things we are to "put on" (see Ephesians 4:17–5:21). Our life is a journey of shedding those things that are part of our sinful nature and adopting those things that are from God.

Every time we respond in obedience to what God reveals as His will through Scripture, we enter a new stage of learning and growing. For instance, I have often talked to congregations about the issue of tithing—giving back to God the first 10 percent of what we earn. While generosity to God is clearly taught in Scripture, the vast majority of people do not tithe. When I ask why, the answer is nearly always, "Because I'm afraid I won't have enough." That is an honest fear and one that I have had a number of times in my own life. So I respond, "Would you be willing to trust God for six months and see what happens?" That is a scary proposition for many people, but at least it has an end point — six months — so most are willing to take the risk.

To their surprise, they discover that God proves Himself faithful. The experience of God actually meeting their needs changes how they think about His provision and their ability to trust Him from that moment on. But it took the risk of obedience to learn the truth. Every act of aligning our lives with God brings growth and greater maturity.

In what ways is God asking you to align your life so that it more closely resembles His? Are you willing to take the steps of obedience, risk, and growth?

LOVE WE GIVE

Regardless of how God has wired us and what our sweet spot is, there is a universal mandate for all of God's people to actively love those around us. Agape love is a very practical love that actively meets the needs of those who come across our path. Love is a powerful accelerator of growth for us and the most powerful sign to those around us of God's mercy and compassion.

Mary Ann and I, along with close friends, learned the power of giving love away early in our marriage. Two days prior to our first Thanksgiving together, I went down to Mickey's Diner (a longtime icon in St. Paul), where lots of poor and down-on-their-luck people would hang out. I told them I would be there at noon on Thanksgiving and would take whoever was interested home to our place for a Thanksgiving dinner.

When I showed up, there were eight people waiting. I brought them back to our small apartment, where Mary Ann and Pam had prepared a feast. We were blown away by how much food those people managed to pile on their plates. Mickey's Diner–type folks are not shy, and we quickly learned that we had assembled quite a variety of people: one of the guys was homeless and cooked canned food on a radiator in a building he frequented; another was a former streetwalker; another was a former police officer who had become an alcoholic; another was a con man who cased our house for valuables (there were none).

After the meal, we had a short devotional and I asked our guests if they wanted to sing any songs. The ones they chose were those they remembered from Sunday school and church years before. Tears streamed down several of the faces as we sang.

It was a surprising afternoon, one we will never forget. It was perhaps the best Thanksgiving we have ever had. I know those people loved the food and having a warm, happy place to celebrate on what would otherwise have been a lonely day. I also know that the experience changed us more than it changed them, which is what happens when we share love in practical ways. It was one of a series of experiences that has given us a lifelong concern for the down-and-out, the poor, and the marginalized.

We have lived in a working-class neighborhood for twenty years. Some of our neighbors live on the margins. There have been many opportunities to show practical love right where we live: cleaning up a rundown house, making a mortgage payment in an emergency, buying groceries for those in need, showing neighbors how to plant a garden, helping build out basements, loving the unloved kids, and coming alongside people in times of crisis.

Each of these acts of love surprised the person who received it because in many cases no one had ever done anything like this for him or her before. What we take for granted in our church fellowships and among Christ followers is foreign to many. We have seen neighbors come to Christ, and others are journeying toward faith. Every time we have an opportunity to show love, we grow and change and God does something significant in our hearts.

Here is the cool thing: Practicing acts of love does not depend on our education, wealth, or ministry training. All of us can and should be living this way. Think of the powerful testimony for Christ, as well as the positive effect on society, if all God's people chose to live lives of active love with those around them. How are you doing in practicing acts of kindness on a regular basis?

COMMUNITY WE PARTICIPATE IN

While we in the United States live in an ultraindividualistic society, the Scriptures indicate that we were not meant to experience life alone. We were meant to share life with other members of the body of Christ—praying for one another, learning from one another, and caring for one another. The key phrase here is "one another," which is used numerous times in the New Testament.

This is why small groups or ministry groups are important in our churches. When I am in a typical church service, I look at the back of people's heads. When I am in a small group, I look at faces as we share life, joys, sorrows, and lessons.

Whether your community is a formal small group or just a group of fellow Christ followers whom you regularly meet with, these are the fundamental building blocks of growth. It may be a men's group or a women's group or a couples' group or a mixed group—each has the "one another" quality that God encourages us to experience. In small and big ways, we grow as we rub shoulders with fellow Christ followers who are pilgrims on the same journey.

THE BOTTOM LINE

Our commitment to keep growing, stay engaged, and join God in His work takes intentionality and a set of disciplines designed to keep us on the growing edge. Our ongoing development is directly related to our legacy and to carrying out the unique role God has for us. It is saying no to complacency and yes to active commitment.

It is also recognizing that as we hone our skills and demonstrate our obedience, our ability to influence others grows and we mature spiritually. And our most significant years should be in our second half, when we have a library of lessons behind us and wisdom that we did not have in the beginning.

REFLECTIVE PRAYER

Father, I desire to finish well, to live out a lifetime of ministry, growth, and engagement. Help me honestly evaluate how well I am doing in staying engaged in nonnegotiated commitment to You. Show me what more I can do to stay on the cutting edge for the sake of the work You have called me to do. Amen.

For Group Discussion

- What factors do you think keep so many believers from staying engaged and continuing to grow in their lives, faith, and ministries?
- Which of the ten growth accelerators discussed in this chapter are easy for you and which are hard? Why?
- What changes do you need to make to continue growing and developing?
- Share a past experience that caused you to grow significantly in your spiritual life.
- Have you taken a significant risk that resulted in growth? Describe the experience and what you learned from it.

Chapter 6

HOW DO I BEST RECHARGE?

Recognizing the Rewards of Refreshment

*When God gives any man wealth and possessions, and enables him
to enjoy them, to accept his lot and be happy in his work — this is a
gift of God. He seldom reflects on the days of his life, because God
keeps him occupied with gladness of heart.*

— Ecclesiastes 5:19-20

One of the best gifts I ever received came years ago when my friend Grant
took me fly-fishing on the Gallatin River in Montana. This is the river
where the wonderful movie *A River Runs Through It* was filmed. It's a
place I've returned to many times since that first introduction.

For the past decade, Mary Ann and I have enjoyed an annual vacation in Montana. All year I look forward to walking the Gallatin and
the nearby streams looking for trout, breathing in the fresh mountain
air, spotting wildlife, enjoying the satisfying exhaustion that comes at
the end of a full day. Montana is where I find extra time to read, write,
watch good movies, and spend time with Mary Ann — all of which bring
refreshment to my mind, body, and soul.

A key requirement of healthy living is ensuring that we get the rest, refreshment, and refueling we need. As Solomon so wisely said, the ability to enjoy the fruits of our labor is a gift of God — not to the exclusion of other priorities, but as one of our key priorities. Why? We cannot run on empty forever. When we try to, we suffer in some way — physically, emotionally, or spiritually.

I consider Grant's teaching me to fly-fish such a great gift because for many years I did not take the issue of refreshment seriously enough. It is still hard for me to slow down, but God used my recent illness to force me to watch my pace more carefully and to be intentional about recharging.

RUNNING ON FUMES

Not long ago I was talking to a friend about a Christian leader who pastored a large church, traveled the country and the globe, wrote books, and spoke to packed crowds. He seemed to have it all together. My friend commented, "He says he is running on fumes."

Within weeks, word hit the national news that this leader's personal life was a mess and that he had lost his ministry. The success, fame, and frenetic pace left too little time for rest, reflection, self-examination, and a needed reality check on the state of his life. His implosion stripped him of what he had built over many years. Running on fumes is a dangerous proposition.

Our bodies and minds were not made to run full speed ahead all the time. If we drive in the red zone of our vehicle's tachometer too long, engine damage will occur. Yet that is often the pace at which we live — at least in the United States. For career people, it is the pace we think we need to keep in order to succeed. For soccer moms, it is keeping up with the demands and schedules of our kids (leaving many kids running on fumes as well). For all of us, the general pace of life can leave our bodies tired and our souls empty.

Rest was intentionally designed into the rhythm of life at the very beginning of creation; God Himself rested on the seventh day. He gave us six days for work and one day for rest, a lost concept in our day. God didn't need the rest, but He knew that those He created would.

If the words *frantic, frazzled,* and *frenzied* describe the pace of your individual life or your family life, take a moment (of rest and reflection) to think about these questions:

- Do you feel refreshed and energized at your current pace?
- What would happen if you just quit doing some of your activities?
- Whose expectations are you trying to live up to with all your pursuits?
- Are your kids getting enough rest and relaxation?
- Do you have time to think strategically about your priorities, schedule, and calling?
- If you could design life, would it be this busy?

We were not designed for frantic lives, nor do we need to live them. When we run too fast, we lose perspective. If we do not build refreshment into our lives, we will not be as productive, satisfied, and fruitful as God desires us to be. The trick is to live with intentionality, paying attention to the important things, including the need for refreshment.

LIFE SATISFACTION

The book of Ecclesiastes is fascinating to read. You can conclude that Solomon was a huge pessimist. "Meaningless! Meaningless! . . . Utterly meaningless! Everything is meaningless" (Ecclesiastes 1:2). Sounds pretty pessimistic to me!

But you need to read on. Solomon's point is that all the work, success, or money in this world will not fulfill us if we have not integrated an eternal purpose into our lives. Later, Paul echoed this theme when he wrote that we were made for relationship with Christ and were gifted to join Him in His work (see Ephesians 2:10). It's not surprising, then, that many successful people in our world are unhappy. They have everything except the one thing they crave: satisfaction. That comes only when we embrace our eternal purpose.

Solomon also said that all the pleasures of the world — and he could speak from experience—were equally meaningless unless they were infused with God's pleasure. Ironically, the toys and experiences pursued by so many are frustrating because the guy with the most toys does not win after all. In themselves, they do not have the ability to bring satisfaction or meaning to life. But if we live our lives with purpose, then both our work and our recreation will be infused with God's joy and satisfaction. That's why Solomon wrote,

> A man can do nothing better than to eat and drink and find satisfaction in his work. This too, I see, is from the hand of God, for without him, who can eat or find enjoyment? To the man who pleases him, God gives wisdom, knowledge and happiness, but to the sinner he gives the task of gathering and storing up wealth to hand it over to the one who pleases God. (Ecclesiastes 2:24-26)

Both work and refreshment are blessed by God when we understand the purpose of our lives—to live in relationship with Him and carry out His unique role for our lives. But the faster we run, the more likely it is that the spiritual component will become lost in the shuffle. In direct correlation to that loss of spiritual connection will be our diminished level of satisfaction and joy.

In a great cosmic irony, the busier we are, the less satisfaction our activities deliver because often the cost of our pace is the loss of meaningful spiritual connection. The faster we go to "get all we can out of life," the less likely we will be to experience that goal. Conversely, the more intentional we are about maintaining a balanced pace, with adequate time to reflect and nurture our spiritual life, the more joy and satisfaction we will experience.

SLOWING DOWN TO HEAR GOD

Those whose lives are most fruitful take the time to think, reflect, dialogue with key friends, and be quiet long enough to hear what God has to tell them. Being more productive in life does not necessarily mean working harder; it means living smarter. It does not mean running faster but rather living wiser at a sustainable pace. It is allowing our minds to be available for greater things.

Consider an episode from the life of the prophet Elijah. He had just come off a tense, dangerous, and stressful time of doing battle with the evil King Ahab. The king had it in for Elijah big-time. Finally, Elijah said to Ahab and his prophets of the pagan god Baal, "Let's see which God is mightier, your Baal or my God." So Ahab assembled all his pagan prophets at Mount Carmel. They put two bulls on the altar, and Elijah said, "You call on the name of your god, and I will call on the name of the LORD. The god who answers by fire — he is God" (1 Kings 18:24).

All day the prophets of Baal frantically called on their god to set the altar on fire, but to no avail. Finally, Elijah repaired the ancient altar to the true God, placed a bull on top, poured water all over it for good measure — three times — and then called on the Lord God. "The fire of the LORD fell and burned up the sacrifice, the wood, the stones and the soil, and also licked up the water in the trench" (18:38).

Wow! Elijah must have been on cloud nine. Not really. These events simply made King Ahab even more intent on killing Elijah, who ran for his life and ended up in Beersheba. Once there, he plopped down under a tree and prayed that he could die. He said to God, "I have had enough" (19:4). God graciously provided Elijah food and water, and the prophet set out on a forty-day walk to Horeb, "the mountain of God," where he went into a cave to spend the night (19:8).

The Lord appeared to Elijah and told him that He was going to pass by. Immediately a

> great and powerful wind tore the mountains apart and shattered the rocks before the LORD, but the LORD was not in the wind. After the wind there was an earthquake, but the LORD was not in the earthquake. After the earthquake came a fire, but the LORD was not in the fire. And after the fire came a gentle whisper. When Elijah heard it, he pulled his cloak over his face and went out and stood at the mouth of the cave. (19:11-13)

And the Lord came and spoke with him.

This account captures my attention because we are often spent and tired like Elijah. We have run the race, accomplished something big or experienced something difficult, and in our exhaustion said, "I've had enough of this!" We wish we could get perspective on our life or situation, and we pray for help and understanding. It took Elijah time alone, in the quiet, to hear God's voice. When it came, it was not in the wind or the earthquake or the fire, but in a gentle whisper. It came when Elijah had stopped long enough to hear his Lord. He was rested and alone and ready to listen.

God often talks to us the same way, in a gentle whisper. To hear a whisper we have to be quiet, free from distraction, and in a place where we can hear and comprehend what God wants to drop into our hearts. It may be an impression, an idea, an understanding, a strategy, or an insight, but the gentle whisper of God gives us what we need in our moment of need.

Does God speak today? Absolutely! We are told by Jesus that His Spirit will guide us into all truth and help us understand the mind of God. But in order to hear the gentle whisper of the Spirit, we need to be quiet long enough so that distractions do not drown out His voice.

God spoke to Mary Ann two days after I was admitted to United Hospital in December 2007. I was struggling to breathe and the prognosis was grave. The physicians did not yet know what they were treating, and I was not responding to the massive antibiotic mixes they were trying. Mary Ann was sitting quietly in my room, watching the pumps and monitors, and asking God how to pray for me.

Then she heard the quiet whisper of God. Clearly, she heard, or felt, God say these words to her: "It will be really close, but he is going to make it."

Moments later, my son Jon walked into the room and said, "Mom, did you feel a sense of peace just come over this place?"

Mary Ann replied, "Yes, and let me tell you why." She told him what the Lord had said to her.

What Mary Ann heard so clearly was highly improbable. A couple of days later, the physicians put me into a coma and on to a ventilator, which I was on for eighteen days. Those days were filled with one crisis after another. There would be small signs of progress, and then I would crash. Over and over. Each time, Mary Ann clung to the promise of God's quiet words.

About a week after my admission, a family meeting was called in the hospital waiting room where my large extended family had gathered (for much of my stay). The doctor shared the bare facts, as he must in situations like that, and left little hope of a positive outcome.

As the doctor left, family members sat lost in their thoughts, their sadness, and the pain of the moment. People started to get up to leave the room, but Mary Ann asked that they stay to pray. During the prayer time she heard God say, "You need to stand up and pray." It became hard for her to be patient while the others prayed because she felt such an urgency to stand and pray and claim God's promise that I would live. That was a risky thing to say in light of the medical facts, but she had heard God's voice and was sticking to His promise. She stood and prayed, "God, I am standing up as a symbol of my confidence that you said T. J. will live, and we are asking for his complete recovery."

From my room Mary Ann could see the St. Paul Cathedral, a beautiful church overlooking the city. On the Sunday afternoon before Christmas, she longed to go there and sit in the quiet, reverent space — alone with God — away from the noise of the machines and the hubbub of clamoring medical staff.

That evening as Mary Ann was eating dinner with some friends and family members at a nearby restaurant, she got an urgent call from my younger sister. "You need to come back. I don't like what I see on the monitor." As she rushed back to the hospital, Mary Ann had a nauseating feeling that this was going to be bad. When she got to my room, my temperature was close to 103 and my heart was racing at an astounding 242 beats per minute. I was in septic shock with a heart valve that was barely functioning; my situation looked dire.

Around the corner from my room was an alcove with a seldom-used telephone desk and some stashed medical equipment. Mary Ann could hide in there and keep an eye on things but still be by herself. The staff hustled Mary Ann out of my room, paged the intensivist ("Stat!"), and started to use the defibrillator ("Clear!") to try to shock my heart back into a survivable rhythm (unsuccessfully).

Amid the frantic activity Mary Ann stayed in the alcove, too overwhelmed to deal with anyone in the waiting room. As she desperately tried to control her stress, God said to her, "This can be your cathedral." He was clearly saying, "I am here. You can be with Me here." And He met her there in the midst of her fear.

To the amazement of the numerous physicians, specialists, and ICU staff, I walked out of the hospital forty-two days after I had arrived. On my way out, we stopped to visit the ICU, where I had spent thirty-two days. The nurse who had used the defibrillator on me said "wow" over and over. She was nearly speechless in her amazement that this was the same person who had been so close to death just weeks earlier.

Does God still speak? Ask Mary Ann. She will tell you He does. But we need to be quiet long enough to hear His voice and receptive enough to believe that the voice is His.

PLACES OF REFRESHMENT

Mary Ann and I have a yurt, one of those tents that folks in Mongolia live in. It is our physical and spiritual retreat on fifteen wonderful acres in western Wisconsin. It is nineteen feet across inside with two recliners, a futon, a wood stove, and some cooking equipment.

We love to escape to the yurt because it is quiet and beautiful. Sometimes I cut trees and brush (chainsaw therapy), and sometimes we just walk the trails or check out Lost Creek, which starts on the property. It is a place of refuge, relaxation, and refreshment. Taking just a few hours to eat a picnic dinner as the sun sets is enough to rejuvenate our souls and reconnect our lives. In the peaceful, quiet setting of those acres, I am able to take a time-out, free my life from distractions, think deeply, and be available to the Spirit's gentle whisper should He want to speak to me.

Because I am by nature someone who runs fast, I have had to learn, as Elijah did, the value and necessity of slowing down to find physical, emotional, and spiritual refreshment. What I have learned is that through refreshment, we actually are able to accomplish a lot more.

In the Gospels we read that Christ would regularly go away alone to pray, meditate, and rest. All of us need places of refreshment where we can recharge. We need places free from distraction where we can hear God's gentle whisper in our hearts. A place of refreshment can be as simple as a room in your home where you can relax, pray, read, and think. For me it is my library, where I can be in a comfy chair near a few hundred of my best friends (books). This is where I tend to write, think, and pray.

What are your places of refreshment where you can get away for even a short time and allow your spirit to be recharged? If you do not have one, take a few moments to think about possible locations that could become your quiet place.

PEOPLE OF REFRESHMENT

Have you noticed that some people drain you and some people fill you? In the last chapter, I talked about the wonderful "friends for life" that Mary Ann and I have. We regularly schedule long dinners with those friends because we never fail to be enriched by the good conversation and genuine encouragement.

God designed us to live and grow in community with others. It is people who make the most profound contributions to our lives and help us keep life in perspective. It is people who demonstrate God's love, grace, and mercy to us in personal ways. We need to be people of refreshment and have key friends who encourage and edify us rather than discourage and deplete us.

This is a great reason to develop close relationships. I enjoy meeting people and have wonderful friends around the world, but it is the deep relationships that have the most power for refreshment and encouragement. I cannot imagine going through any major decision or event in my life without the input and insight of my closest friends.

The individualism of our culture runs counter to these kinds of deep, meaningful relationships. People in our society are often too busy, too private, and too wary to develop soul-mate relationships. I enjoy traveling to places like the Middle East, Lebanon, Israel, and Egypt, where the highlight of the day is the noon or evening meal with friends and family. It is common for these mealtimes to last for hours. Their culture understands friendships and the value of time spent together over great food. Interestingly, one of the descriptions we have of heaven revolves around a banquet table (see Revelation 19:9).

Deep friendship requires a willingness and trust to share our lives together, knowing that we are safe in disclosing who we are and what we are going through. (Of course, some people are not safe, so we need to be discerning.) It is a great gift to be able to share yourself freely with trusted friends without having to hide parts of your life.

Who are the people of refreshment in your life? Do you make time for these relationships on a regular basis?

PRACTICES THAT REFRESH

There are also practices that bring refreshment to us. Each of us needs consistent outlets that help us release stress, renew our energy, and create the space necessary to contemplate. For me, doing something physical, though at a leisurely pace, helps me recharge. Whether it is fly-fishing, cutting trees, or walking, I do my best thinking when I am expending energy on activities that fill my tank.

My son Steven does his best thinking when he is making something, whether in his forge in the backyard or in the woodworking room at Bethel University. As an artist, he processes his thoughts and gets in his zone while exercising his creativity.

I have other friends who use eighteen holes of golf to refresh. Some recharge with one or two other people over coffee, sharing their lives with trusted friends. Our friend Barb loves to walk and does a lot of thinking and praying on her daily hike. Carol's passion is gardening, and she does her reflecting while pulling weeds and pinching buds.

While all of us have our own recreational pursuits to help us recharge, there's another activity that we should take better advantage of: reading the Scriptures. The psalmist affirmed the Bible's ability to restore us: "My soul is weary with sorrow; strengthen me according to your word" (119:28). Later in the same chapter he wrote, "Your statutes are wonderful; therefore I obey them. The unfolding of your words gives light; it gives understanding to the simple" (verses 129-130).

Few practices will provide more refreshment to tired hearts than regularly soaking in the words of our Father found in Scripture. Reading the Bible is not an obligation to be endured but a dialogue to be savored and enjoyed. After all, we are communicating with the God of the universe, who loves us endlessly and speaks to us through His Word. It is amazing how a few minutes in God's Word can quiet our minds, correct our perspective, give us hope, and point us in directions that are life-giving rather than life-draining. As the psalmist went on to say, "Great peace have they who love your law, and nothing can make them stumble" (verse 165).

What are the activities that you really enjoy that allow you to refresh your spirit and think deeply? Do you give yourself adequate time with those activities so that you are able to think, reflect, and allow the Spirit to talk to you about the issues of life? Do you regularly absorb the inspiration found in God's Word?

PERSONAL RETREAT TIME

We have talked about the importance of living intentionally, setting priorities, and making time for refreshment. For years I have tried to apply these principles with the help of a monthly personal retreat. (Yours might be monthly, quarterly, biannually, or some other regular interval.)

A personal retreat is time set aside to think, pray, plan, meditate, journal, and read. In order for this to be meaningful time, distractions are a no-no. That means television, radio, your cell phone, and e-mail are off-limits. Keep your journal handy to record any impressions or insights that come to you. The location should be someplace where you can relax, think, and be free of interruption.

During my retreats I review my priorities and assess how I am doing with each of them and whether I need to make changes. I scrutinize my schedule to ensure that it aligns with my priorities. I pray about opportunities and seek God's wisdom regarding my response. Above all, I spend time quietly giving God's Spirit the chance to drop things into my heart that would be helpful to my work, ministry, and personal life. When I first started incorporating a personal retreat on a monthly basis, I thought, *I don't have time to do this.* Now, after years of experience, I've concluded that I don't have time *not* to do this.

GOD CARES ABOUT *WHO* WE ARE, NOT *WHAT* WE DO

Though we live in a performance-oriented society, God's perspective is that who we are and who we become is more important than what we do and what we accomplish. It is not that our work and activities are unimportant—on the contrary. But much more important than our performance is the *person* we truly are.

Because of society's pressure, many of us are overcommitted. But following Christ frees us from the need to constantly do more to win approval and acceptance. There is nothing you can do to make God love you any more or any less than He does right now. God's love is constant and we cannot win it. He offers it freely to those who will say yes to His offer to be the Lord of their lives.

He wants us to embrace His call on our lives and fulfill His assignment for us. We don't do that by trying harder but by living with intentionality and inviting Him to change our hearts in the process.

The healthier we are emotionally, spiritually, and physically, the more productive we will be. There is no way to microwave health. It is easy to ignore and hard to quantify. Others don't necessarily see our emotional or spiritual health until neglect causes problems in our lives. What people see of us is like an iceberg, a small portion of who we really are. Our thoughts, motives, intentions, intimacy with Christ (or lack thereof), and habits that we practice (or don't) are the powerful but hidden core of who we are. These things form the character that flows out of us. Too often we focus on looking good rather than on the hidden character that needs to be transformed. The public us is only an extension of the private us. Character is what we are when no one is looking—and character is formed in the dark before it is exposed in the light.

Jesus regularly withdrew "to a solitary place, where he prayed" and spent time with the Father (Mark 1:35). How often do we follow His example? Is there space in our busy lives to do "soul work," allowing God to mold our thinking, priorities, passions, and innermost heart? Is your private life robust and healthy or anorexic and feeble? The answer to that question will contribute to your success or failure more than any other issue. Building times of refreshment into our lives is fundamental to ensuring that we give ourselves and the Spirit opportunity to keep our hidden selves healthy so that who we are informs and strengthens what we do.

THE BOTTOM LINE

Everywhere I go, people tell me life is too busy. For most of us, it is—and such an unbalanced life is detrimental to our emotional, spiritual, and physical well-being. As our spirits become eroded over time, our effectiveness wanes and the joy and satisfaction that Solomon referred to are diminished.

That is why the question "How do I best recharge?" is one of the ten most important questions you could ever ponder. Making times of refreshment a priority is critical to clearer, deeper thinking, to keeping one's heart attuned to God, and to physical and emotional health. For the person who wants to live intentionally, joyfully, and effectively, this is a nonnegotiable.

REFLECTIVE PRAYER

Father, I thank You that You designed us for balanced lives, where we can find joy and satisfaction in our work and in those things that renew and refresh us. Remind me often that who I am is more important than what I do. Give me the joy and satisfaction described by Solomon in abundance as I integrate You into my work and my times of refreshment. Amen.

For Group Discussion

- Tell about the places, people, and practices that bring you refreshment, allow you to think deeply, and enable you to hear the promptings of God's Spirit.
- How do you balance work, schedules, and obligations with regular times of refreshment? Are there modifications you need to make in order to live a more balanced life?
- What can we learn about life and satisfaction from Solomon's words (see Ecclesiastes 5:18-20)?
- If you have ever heard the quiet voice of God, share what happened. How did the experience affect you?

Chapter 7

HOW CAN MY LIFE HAVE A RIPPLE EFFECT?

Initiating Ways to Influence and Inspire Others

When [Saul, later to be named Paul] came to Jerusalem, he tried to join the disciples, but they were all afraid of him, not believing that he really was a disciple. But Barnabas . . . told them how Saul on his journey had seen the Lord and that the Lord had spoken to him, and how in Damascus he had preached fearlessly in the name of Jesus. So Saul stayed with them and moved about freely in Jerusalem, speaking boldly in the name of the Lord.

— Acts 9:26-28

In steamy Manila, I sat in a hotel lobby with a couple I'll call Andrew and Beth. They were in the Philippines attending graduate school but were citizens of Myanmar (formerly Burma), a beautiful country bordered by Thailand, India, Laos, Bangladesh, and China. It is a place of great natural resources, but because of its brutal military regime, the country is under international sanctions, resulting in unemployment and poverty.

My introduction to Andrew and Beth was through a colleague of mine who had mentored Andrew over a number of years in the Philippines. Andrew had just completed his graduate work and was ready to return to Myanmar, except for the fact that he did not have the money for a ticket to get back home. I told him our organization would help.

I saw huge potential in this couple. They had hearts for reaching Myanmar with the good news of Jesus Christ and for helping people get out of poverty, gain an education, and become self-sufficient. As I listened and interacted with them, I kept thinking, *These are wonderful people. I want to get involved in their lives, be an advocate for them, and help them become everything they can be.*

Thus started what is now a five-year relationship that has led me to travel to Myanmar to meet with Andrew and to rendezvous with him in other parts of Asia and in the United States. I have had the privilege of being one of Andrew's mentors, along with a number of others who have seen the same potential. Andrew had been living in Yangon, the former capital of Burma, where life was hard but livable compared to other parts of the country. He dreamed of going to more remote places in his country to share the gospel, train leaders, and establish holistic ministries. That is no easy task since some villages in Myanmar are a three-day walk from the nearest road. Travel can be extra difficult because transportation is unreliable and military checkpoints dot the roads.

Then in April 2008, disaster struck Myanmar in the form of a devastating cyclone that ripped through the low-lying delta area, killing more than 100,000 people (many of whom were simply swept out to sea from the tidal surge). The disaster also left more than one million people homeless, without food or drinkable water, and with their farmland ruined.

The world watched as many governments and agencies stood ready to help, but the military junta of Myanmar would not let them in. When, precious weeks after the disaster, they finally started to let some aid in, much of it disappeared into the junta's hands. Most heartrending was that the junta would not allow its own citizens to travel to the devastated delta region to provide aid. The leaders wanted to be seen as the all-powerful "parent" of the citizens of Myanmar.

For Andrew and Beth, this was the opportunity their hearts had been waiting for. Andrew started making secret trips to the delta in order to see what could be done. Soon he was handing out food and water and helping people rebuild their homes. But the undertaking was massive.

Our staff in Asia quickly came alongside Andrew and Beth, coached them on developing a team, provided resources from relief funds, and worked behind the scenes to help them launch a new ministry. It's an organization operating in a country that makes such ministries illegal.

Last week I read Andrew's monthly report. They now run a ministry center in a village in the delta, hold classes for children, rebuild homes, dig wells, help families get back on their feet, and train women to sew so they can make a livelihood. Andrew and Beth have seen many become Christ followers as they experienced the love of these Christians. I live for these kinds of opportunities because one of the most significant things we can do is create a ripple that spreads outward in concentric circles, on and on and on. It is the stuff legacy is made of.

MADE TO RIPPLE

Drop a pebble in a pond and what happens? One splash creates ripples that reverberate across the surface in ever-widening circles. Drop a bunch of pebbles in a pond and the various ripples hit one another and create small waves that start moving the whole surface. It is the nature of influence.

The most important work we do for Christ is that of creating ripples for Him. Christ created ripples with His disciples, who created ripples with new believers in Jerusalem, who in turn created ripples with the whole world as they were forced out of town by persecution and ended up on the highways and byways of the Roman Empire. All these ripples of influence collaborated to change the course of civilization forever.

If Barnabas had not come alongside Paul when the other apostles were frightened of him, Paul's ministry would not have gotten off to the start it did. Likewise, Paul created ripples with Timothy and Titus and numerous other leaders in the early church.

Someone created ripples with my friend Andrew when he was young, and he became a Christ follower. Another created ripples by making it possible for him to get a theological and social-work degree. Friends of mine created more ripples by providing counsel and encouragement along the way. Now Andrew and Beth create ripples in the delta and across Myanmar with the gospel and with tangible help. See how the ripples are multiplying across borders and into places that most of us would never be able to visit?

The reason God gives spiritual gifts to every Christ follower is to allow us to create ripples of influence and life change. Whether it is teaching, healing, prayer, administration, leadership, care, giving, encouraging, or a whole host of other ways, we have been gifted. These gifts are given so that we can influence others in the church and the world for Him. One splash, many ripples!

My mother-in-law was a simple woman. Originally from Sweden, she came to the United States by ship and got so seasick that she swore she would never go back. She met her future husband in English class in St. Paul. He was an immigrant from the Ukraine, having lived through the Second World War, where he served in the Russian, German, and American armies (his is a long and amazing story worth a book in itself).

My father-in-law never learned English very well, and for the first five years I dated Mary Ann, I just said yes to every question he asked—not always understanding what he was saying. I guess it was the right thing to say because when I asked his permission to marry his daughter, he said the same thing back.

Gunberg, my mother-in-law, served as a nurse's aide at a local hospital. She also spent thousands of hours with her four grandchildren, two of them ours. In 1997 Gunberg was in a car accident that, a month later, claimed her life. We were moved by how many came to her memorial service. She had never served on a committee in the church or had any visible ministry. But we heard story after story from people who had benefited from her small acts of kindness: making meals, visiting, sewing clothes, giving money, helping neighbors, praying, and offering encouragement. She was not a theologian, had few resources, worked a modest-paying job, and was a first-generation immigrant, yet she touched a lot of people — no doubt part of the reason my wife and sons also have a heart for the underdog.

All over the world I meet individuals like my mother-in-law who are quietly and effectively loving people and demonstrating small acts of kindness. Why do I think a lot of these will be at the front of the line when we get to heaven? They are people who quietly but intentionally create ripples as a way of life.

Karen, who personally knows the pain that women who have had abortions live with, started a ministry called Deeper Still, a weekend experience to bring healing and wholeness to ravaged hearts.[1] Every weekend that she conducts a retreat, she creates ripples in hurting hearts. Newly healed hearts then leave and help other hurting hearts.

As Ellen works with AIDS orphans in Thailand, she creates ripples of love, hope, and happiness, along with ripples of the gospel. Those children and women will never be the same and will go on to help other hurting kids and women. Those who minister among the poor, hungry, forgotten, needy, jobless, and drug addicted are true heroes because this is right where the heart of God is (see Isaiah 58).

Most of us are rather ordinary people. We do not possess great resources or wealth. We have average jobs and income. We are not famous or well known. But all of us have the one thing that we need to make ripples for Christ: We are surrounded by the people He wants us to influence. While the world pursues things and bank accounts and prestige and properties, God and His people pursue people. Stuff will not outlast our world, but every human being has an eternal destiny, either with God or without Him.

My niece Mandie will be a high school senior this coming year. Academics are not easy for Mandie, and she is quiet and somewhat shy. But she loves to help others. Just before graduation at a local alternative school, she stayed up most of the night, helping academically challenged students finish their work so they could graduate. A small thing? Actually, it was a small act of love that had huge implications for those who, without her help, could not have graduated. She created ripples in a big way.

Who are the people within your sphere of influence for whom you can intentionally create ripples? How can you use your gifts and the opportunities God gives to cause the circles to spread?

A WAY OF SEEING

Perspective and vision are interesting things. Two eyewitnesses of an accident can both see the same thing but report different scenarios. As Christ followers, we are constantly challenged to see life, circumstances, events, and news from an eternal perspective rather than a human perspective.

There is an account in the Gospels where Jesus and the disciples were overwhelmed by crowds of people eager to meet Jesus and desperate to have their circumstances changed. The disciples were tired and saw the crowds as a distraction and a hassle. But Jesus had a different response: "When he saw the crowds, he had compassion on them, because they were harassed and helpless, like sheep without a shepherd" (Matthew 9:36). The disciples saw from human eyes while Jesus saw with kingdom eyes.

Human sight is at its core selfish. It sees those things that help or hinder us, are to our advantage or disadvantage, give us power or rob us of it. Kingdom sight is utterly unselfish. It is about giving rather than receiving and serving rather than being served.

There is also a time perspective to human versus kingdom seeing. Human eyes are concerned about how the circumstances of life affect us. Kingdom eyes are concerned about how the circumstances of life build God's kingdom, even if to our temporary detriment. Kingdom seeing keeps eternity in mind, viewing life from God's perpsective.

How we view people around us depends on which eyes we see them through. From a human perspective, many people are simply losers who have little value to us or to society. They may lack the education, sophistication, status, or whatever it is that gives one value in our world. Kingdom vision sees the same people and perceives them as precious to God and enormously valuable.

Which way of seeing is your default? Can you think of instances when you saw through human eyes and other instances when you saw through kingdom eyes?

A WAY OF LOVING

The second skill we need to learn in order to create positive ripples is to love people as Jesus loved them. He met their needs, expressed compassion, extended grace, and befriended sinners, prostitutes, and outcasts. His ministry was actually more on Skid Row than on Easy Street. The reason bad or poor or marginalized people responded to Him was that He offered love rather than judgment, grace rather than condemnation, and hope rather than pessimism. He made sure they knew that they were valued, precious in God's sight.

One of the most powerful acts of love comes when we extend unexpected or undeserved grace to another. Our world has a "you get what you have coming" attitude and is often judgmental and unforgiving. It does not know how to respond to forgiveness and grace. Even Christ followers are guilty of shooting their wounded rather than extending forgiveness and grace to one another.

The gospel of Christ is fundamentally different from other world religions in the unconditional, freely given nature of salvation. Instead of having to earn God's favor or needing to do penance for our sin, God simply extends to us His forgiveness and grace. The apostle Paul put it this way:

> Like the rest, we were by nature objects of wrath. But because of his great love for us, God, who is rich in mercy, made us alive with Christ even when we were dead in transgressions. . . . It is by grace you have been saved, through faith — and this not from yourselves, it is the gift of God — not by works, so that no one can boast. (Ephesians 2:3-5,8-9)

The gospel rocked the establishment in Paul's day because it did not make sense. The prevailing belief said, "The gift of forgiveness and grace cannot be free. Nothing is free. Certainly, we must do something to earn it or something to deserve it." But we can do neither. That is the nature and definition of grace; it is undeserved and unearned favor that

God extends to any who will accept it.

Consider the shock of the religious leaders of Christ's day when the worst of sinners accepted His gift and were welcomed by Him into His kingdom. Talk about ripples—and controversy! When we extend love and acceptance to those around us, the same kinds of ripples are set in motion.

THE AMAZING POWER OF GRACE

Think about the people you really love to be around who accept you for who you are, stick by you in tough times, and do not act judgmentally. Friends like these are magnets because you don't have to prove yourself to them; they just love you for who you are. Those who grew up in homes where performance was emphasized and conditional love was prevalent know what I am talking about. Unconditional love is like a cool oasis in a dry desert.

This is why Jesus was such a magnet for people who had screwed up their lives. The more we need forgiveness, the more we appreciate grace. And Jesus extended grace to those who never expected it and, from the perspective of the religious authorities, did not deserve it.

People crave the unconditional love Jesus gave to those around Him. Because of His grace and love, He could call people to righteousness and repentance, and they listened. When people respond to the good news of the gospel, the Holy Spirit starts to work in their lives. He (not us) convicts them of sin and unrighteousness and plants in their hearts a desire to live like Jesus.

As a school nurse, Mary Ann was called the "second mom" by a lot of troubled students. Those who came to school hungry knew that she had a stash of food for them in the closet. Those who were trapped in bad relationships knew they could talk to her. Those who became pregnant knew that she would love them. I remember one time when she brought a birthday cake to school for a troubled young lady and told her to get her friends together for a party. This sixteen-year-old had never had a birthday party in her life. Stunned, she didn't know who to invite.

Here is the fascinating thing: Mary Ann can be blunt and truthful with these kids about dangerous and destructive behaviors, and they never mind because she demonstrates such unconditional love and grace for them. She is not perceived as judgmental but rather as someone who is in their corner and looking out for them. So even after repeatedly screwing up, they can come back because in Mary Ann they find security, love, grace, and truth.

This is what Jesus offered. The apostle John wrote in John 1:17 that "the law was given through Moses; grace and truth came through Jesus Christ." That is a powerful balance for any of us who want to create ripples. Anyone who has that combination of grace and truth becomes a magnet for people who are vulnerable and in pain.

How would you rate yourself in the areas of grace and truth toward those around you? Think about a time when you got it right and an instance when you got it wrong.

FISHERS OF MEN

Recall the words Jesus used when He called His disciples: "Come, follow me . . . and I will make you fishers of men" (Matthew 4:19). The purpose of His incarnation—His appearance on earth as a human being—was to introduce men and women to Himself and bring hope to a sinful world. That becomes the purpose of everyone who follows Him.

We make the concept of evangelism way too complicated, as if it requires special training or is limited to a few. Remember that these disciples who became "fishers of men" and leaders in the early church were ordinary folk. They were not trained theologians; they simply had experienced a relationship with the living God and were compelled to share the new life they had found with others.

Think about how we share our lives with friends. We talk about the weather, interests, politics, sports, the economy, our kids, and our jobs. Why not also talk about our faith, which in the end is the most important and central aspect of our lives? All of us meet people who are facing challenges. Mary Ann and I often simply say to troubled individuals, "We would love to pray for you." And we do. That allows us to follow up and ask how things are going.

We have found that when we do this, God shows up in the lives of the hurting people, and the next time they face a challenge, they ask us to pray again. Often we reply, "Sure, but you know you can pray as well. God will hear your prayers just as He hears ours." Soon those people are on a journey toward faith in Christ. Ripples! When God answers prayer, it leads to more substantive conversations about what it means to trust and follow Jesus. We've seen many people come to faith because of this simple act of obedience.

Neither Mary Ann nor I claim to have the gift of evangelism. But we are still witnesses, fishers of men and women who want to start positive ripples by sharing the good news of Jesus. That is what every Christ follower is called to do in his or her everyday life. Being a fisher of men, in the footsteps of Jesus and the apostles and Christians down through the centuries, is simply being willing to share one's faith in practical ways. Those whose hearts are open will want to know more, which leads them to faith—and the cycle starts all over again.

Has God allowed you to lead others to faith in Jesus? Are there people in your circle you could be open with about your faith in nonthreatening ways? Write down their names and start to pray that God would give you an opportunity to share hope with them.

BEING AN OPEN BOOK

If you want to have influence, one of the greatest gifts you can give to those around you is to be an open book. This means living a life of authenticity, open to the scrutiny of others, with no need to pretend you are something you are not. It is a "what you see is what you get" approach to life. Authenticity is a rare commodity because we often feel a need to present a public face to others that portrays what we think Christians should look like (whatever that is). Simply listen to the conversation in many churches and ask yourself, *Are people really being open and honest about their joys, sorrows, struggles, and challenges?*

This past year has been an interesting one for our family as thousands have prayed for us during and after my forty-two-day hospital stay. Our candid disclosure of our needs and situation was forced on us by events beyond our control. But many people have thanked us for our level of transparency.

Indeed, transparency is a gift we give to others because people can relate to real-life struggles much more than they can to squeaky-clean facades. It is a gift to those who are not yet following Christ when they can watch Christ followers struggle with real issues of life balanced by imperfect but genuine faith. The more open we are, the more approachable we are. The more approachable we are, the more influence we will have with those around us. The cost is admitting that we are not perfect, that our families are not perfect, and that we don't have it all figured out. People who give the gift of being an open book ripple in an especially powerful way.

When talking to medical personnel about my serious illness and miraculous recovery, we always mention our conviction that it was because of the prayers of so many that God healed me. These professionals understand what we are saying because they have no other explanation. Knowing the gravity of my illness and the medical impossibility of my recovery, they cannot say much except to acknowledge that there was outside intervention. All God wants from us is transparency about real life and real faith.

Every challenge comes with the opportunity for us to respond with openness, and every time we do, we have a chance to create faith ripples. People watch and are intrigued by those whose faith carries them through tough times.

My friend Doug, to whom this book is dedicated, had a very wide circle of friends. He was a real guy who faced real situations with his family, his business, and his health. The faith and conviction that he demonstrated in tough situations were a huge witness to others. He did not gloss over those challenges but met them with trust in God. His final battle with ALS was a testimony to his faith, watched and admired by many. He was honest about his fears, disappointments, and desire for healing—but greater than any of these was his absolute faith in the goodness and trustworthiness of God. That transparency was a gift to all of us, and the impact of his life and death and faith sent out ripples of influence that will continue for a long time.

How transparent are you with your life, struggles, and faith? How have you found your transparency to be received by others?

THE GIFT OF MENTORING

Another excellent way to start faith ripples is to mentor others. Once I hit the age of fifty, I knew that the greatest legacy I could leave would be the people I could significantly influence. This includes raising up the next generation of leaders in the organization I serve as well as others in whom I see significant potential.

On a regular basis I mentor, either formally or informally, at least ten individuals. Generally this means meeting with them for an hour or two each month, sometimes via video where we can see each other on a screen and sometimes face-to-face over lunch or coffee. I ask the individual what is on his mind, what God has been doing in his life, or what struggles he has been having. Then, in dialogue form, I ask questions designed to help him think and reflect well.

At first I wondered how it would go with a fiftysomething guy trying to relate to a younger individual. I learned that young people today are hungry for someone to share their experiences and help them think through the issues of life and how God wants to use them. A mentoring ministry has become one of my life passions because when I come alongside people, the ripples of my influence ripple on into their relationships with others. The impact is greater than I will know this side of eternity.

Everyone reading this book has the potential to mentor others, regardless of your age or your personal situation:

- Women can mentor other women.
- Men can mentor other men.
- Adults can mentor young people.

- Young people can mentor young people.
- Executives can mentor other executives.
- Couples can mentor other couples.

It does not have to be formal; if you will spend time with the other person, get to know him or her, ask good questions, and share your life, your encouragement and experience will rub off.

Are there people, young or not so young, you could come alongside and influence through a mentoring relationship over time? In your journal or in a notebook write down their names so you don't forget and ask God for opportunities to begin this process.

STRATEGIC RIPPLES

All ripples are important. Some can be truly strategic. It is a matter of thinking how we can multiply ourselves. Christ followers in Congo became burdened for the tens of thousands of orphans there due to the AIDS epidemic. They did not want to create orphanages where kids were taken out of a home setting and away from their town or village. They also knew that orphanages can be expensive to maintain. So they partnered with Christ followers in the United States. What came from these connections was the organization GlobalFingerprints, which places AIDS orphans in the homes of Christian families in the orphans' own village. The monthly contribution from those in the States who sponsor each orphan pays for their food and education. The stories of these kids are absolutely amazing.[2]

I have shared the incredible story of Heartland Community Church in Rockford, Illinois. One of the goals of this church is to bless the entire city of Rockford and to find ways to send ripples of God's love throughout the city. A few years ago, members of the church approached city leaders to ask if there were schools in need of renovation. At first the city leaders didn't take them seriously, but the church members kept asking until the city gave them a list of priorities.

Thus was born the first Share Fest of Heartland Community Church.

During Easter break of 2008 nearly four thousand people mobilized from three partner churches to give thirty thousand man-hours renovating three schools. Those involved raised $200,000 for the project from many sources, including forty-two corporate sponsors. The city of Rockford had never seen anything like this happen before.

Think of the ripples that went out as thousands of Christ followers came together to do something that would touch every child and every family associated with those schools. Share Fest has become an annual event, and numerous businesses in Rockford now partner with Heartland in providing financial gifts or gifts in kind. In addition, Heartland hosts a citywide mentoring program for inner-city kids.

No matter how God wired you or how He gifted you, His strategy for bringing bits of heaven to earth is very simple. He has placed each of us in a sphere of influence that is unique to us, and He's given us opportunities others don't have. It may be your neighborhood, place of employment, social circle, or any number of unique circumstances. God's desire is for each of us to use our resources and talents to send ripples of His love moving outward.

PICTURE THIS

A day is coming when each of us will stand before our wonderful heavenly Father. We will realize then that a lot of things we thought were important really were not. No longer will our job title, social network, bank account, home, or toys mean anything. Just being with Jesus will mean everything.

As the shock of the moment sets in, we will look around and see all kinds of people we know smiling at us, thanking us, embracing us, and greeting us by name. The crowd will start to grow until we realize that these are all the people we influenced during our lifetime. Names we had long forgotten will come back, and acts of kindness and love will be remembered. Some will come up and introduce themselves and tell the story of how our influence on someone else had a ripple effect on their lives — and how thankful they are that we were faithful. Or they will tell us about the project we helped fund that resulted in their finding Christ.

We will realize more fully than ever before that this is what mattered—these people and the ripples of our lives that had results far beyond our wildest expectations. And we will look back into the loving eyes of Jesus, see a smile on His face, and instantly know that our efforts were well worth it.

When that day comes, I want to know my life has had a ripple effect with:

- My relationships
- My sphere of influence
- The money I invested in ministry
- The use of the gifts God gave me
- A crowd of people with whom I will spend eternity

THE BOTTOM LINE

Each of us has an assignment from God and each of us has specific gifts. But here is the heart of the matter: We are to use our gifting, opportunities, and relationships to send ripples of His love and grace throughout the world, just as Jesus did. He took our sins on Himself, died on the cross, and paid the penalty for our sins. Our opportunity is to create ripples on His behalf, and together we will see the ripples of our lives move in ever-widening circles in our neighborhoods, places of work, communities, and the globe.

We will see amazing legacy from our ripples. When we choose to throw our stones into the pond and start the waves moving, we are living at the intersection of God's call on our lives and our willingness to embrace that call.

REFLECTIVE PRAYER

Father, I thank You for everyone whose ripples influenced my spiritual life and growth. Reveal to me those You want me to love and care for on Your behalf. I ask for wisdom, empowerment, and favor with people so that the ripples I make for You are eternal. Amen.

For Group Discussion

- As you think back on your life, can you think of a ripple of God's love that started elsewhere but touched your life?
- Think about your current sphere of influence. In what ways can you start ripples moving outward in the unique place God has put you?
- How are you doing to develop the two skills of Jesus: seeing people as He sees them and loving people as He loves them?
- Share an experience where God clearly used you to create a ripple effect.

Chapter 8

HOW DO I RELATE TO GOD?

DEEPENING YOUR SPIRITUAL CONNECTION

I am the way and the truth and the life. No one comes to the Father except through me.

— JOHN 14:6

The great lie of the evil one is that life is about *us*—when in truth we were created by God to be in relationship with Him and to join Him in His work. Life is about God, not us. But God does not force us to recognize that. We make the choice, and the choice we make has eternal consequences.

There is much talk these days about spirituality, and a common view is that we do not need to hold to certain beliefs so long as we are *spiritual*—that's enough to know God. The variety of such spiritual paths is amazingly diverse, and if they include the Bible, they also include other holy books or popular works by spiritual experts, all promoting their path to enlightenment.

This quest for spiritual understanding is a remnant of life as God intended it, before Adam and Eve chose to go their own way. As men and women made in the image of God, even though broken and out of relationship with Him, we long for something of Him in our search for spiritual wholeness.

While God has made Himself known to mankind from the beginning of time, a dilemma remains: How can one know a God who cannot be seen or touched? How can sinners relate to a God who is so holy that it is impossible to be in His presence? How does a human relate to a Spirit? How does a mortal relate to the eternal Creator of all things, who started history and who will end history by inaugurating an eternal kingdom? Most of all, how do we deal with the all-pervasive problem of sin, which separates us from this majestic and holy God?

THE INCARNATION

There is no story more beautiful than that of the incarnation of Jesus Christ. We have trivialized the Incarnation into a nice holiday season with presents and fancy trees, when the reality was stark and harsh. The Son of God, the One who was present at the creation of the world, the One whom mankind rejected to go their own way, the King of the universe, was willingly sent by the Father to become a baby in a squalid town, Bethlehem, and to grow up in a working-class home building furniture. Think of that—the One who had made the world, the mountains, the seas, the animals, the sky, and the galaxies began sawing wood to make tables and chairs.

By becoming human, by taking on our humanity, Christ changed the way we could relate to God. Becoming like us and living with us for a season, He enabled us to touch, hear, learn from, and relate to the unapproachable God. The apostle John put it this way: "The Word became flesh and made his dwelling among us. We have seen his glory, the glory of the One and Only, who came from the Father, full of grace and truth" (John 1:14). Never again could men and women say, "I cannot understand God," for now they had met—and can continue to meet—the Lord of the universe in the person of Jesus Christ.

When Jesus started His ministry at age thirty, He was clear about one thing: The only way to the Father, the only way to salvation, was through

Him. "I am the way and the truth and the life. No one comes to the Father except through me" (John 14:6). There are no alternate routes, no other spiritual guides. He and He alone is the route to the Father.

This is not politically correct, of course, and never has been. Reading the Gospels and Paul's letters, you discover that it was not well accepted in that day either. For the religious officials in Judea, Jesus could not be the awaited Messiah because he came in poverty and died on a cross in shame. For the Greeks and Romans, with all their various New Age religions including statues to unknown gods, a Savior who died and rose again was nothing less than foolishness on a grand scale.

In our day, Christianity is vilified, legislated against, and ignored, while alternate spiritual routes are explored and embraced—no matter that they contradict one another and have no basis in truth. I am intrigued by how quickly people grab on to various spiritual routes that have no validity in history and no internal consistency, only vague and foggy spiritual language.

We said that the lie of the evil one is that life is about us. There is another lie: that we can choose our path to God. This is a grand lie indeed since it attempts to elevate our wisdom above God's and allows us to create our own god, our own path, and our own spirituality. This is an even greater lie than the first one because now not only is life not about us but we also have the ability to determine its destiny.

If Jesus was trying to create a popular religion, He failed miserably. God would not appear as a baby, make furniture, live itinerantly without a home, and befriend prostitutes and the sick and the poor and sinners. He would not allow Himself to be nailed to a cross so He could bear our sin. He would not choose twelve followers who wouldn't qualify for anything other than average jobs and tell them to change the world. He would not choose ordinary people like us down through the centuries to keep on changing the world.

Or would He?

Jesus did not come as a religious guru or to found a pop religion. He came as the Lord of the universe, took on our flesh, and with truth and grace pointed us to Himself as the One who could save us from our sin and give hope to the hopeless. Jesus and the message of the gospel have been transforming individual lives, one at a time, ever since. Not through religion, but through relationship with Him.

Anyone who is serious about a relationship with Jesus Christ must confront His claim that He is the only way to the Father. There are no alternate routes. If He was wrong on that, then He is not God. If He was right on that, then He is indeed the only way to God.

FAITH

How do we enter into relationship with Him? Simply by faith—by acknowledging we are sinners who need forgiveness, believing in Him as God's Son and Savior, and asking Him to enter our lives. Paul wrote,

> But because of his great love for us, God, who is rich in mercy, made us alive with Christ even when we were dead in transgressions. . . . It is by grace you have been saved, through faith—and this not from yourselves, it is the gift of God—not by works, so that no one can boast. (Ephesians 2:4-5,8-9)

And here is another of the great improbables that has made many uncomfortable with the gospel of Christ: Salvation is absolutely free, and we can do nothing to deserve or earn or pay for it. Jesus said, "Whoever believes in the Son has eternal life" (John 3:36). Period. It was Jesus Himself who said, "For God so loved the world that he gave his one and only Son, that whoever believes in him shall not perish but have eternal life" (John 3:16). I am a child of God not because I deserve to be, not because of anything I have done, not because of my goodness—but because of my faith in Jesus as my Savior and the only One who can and has forgiven my sin.

JESUS: THE DIVIDING LINE OF HISTORY

When Jesus rose from the dead, He did so as a man with nail holes in His hands and feet. Yes, His body was now an eternal body, for He could walk through doors and appear and disappear—yet He could also eat and talk and fellowship with those to whom He appeared.

In the same way, we're told a day will come when our earthly bodies will be transformed into heavenly bodies just like Christ's. The apostle Paul wrote,

> But our citizenship is in heaven. And we eagerly await a Savior from there, the Lord Jesus Christ, who, by the power that enables him to bring everything under his control, will transform our lowly bodies so that they will be like his glorious body. (Philippians 3:20-21)

The Creator did not just take on flesh and bone; He took on a human body (now a heavenly body but human in form) for all eternity. When you go to heaven, you will meet the same Jesus who walked this earth and rose from the dead, and you will recognize Him by the nail holes in His hands. Why is this significant? Because Jesus has chosen to identify with us so fully that He took on our nature—the form of those He created—forever.

AMAZING GRACE

One cannot understand a relationship with Jesus without understanding the power and the scandal of grace. Reading the Gospels, you encounter Jesus at every juncture healing the sick and declaring even the most sinful of people forgiven. Just like that! They needed it; they requested it; and He willingly gave it. Never, when someone asked to be forgiven, did He refuse to forgive.

How many of us carry guilt for past decisions that we wish we could undo? Jesus says, "I forgive you. Enter into My grace." How many of us have secrets that have burdened us for years? Jesus says, "I forgive you. Enter into My grace." How many of us feel unworthy of a friendship with Him? Jesus says, "I forgive you; I love you; and I died for you. Enter into My grace."

That is the scandal of grace. There is no past that Jesus will not willingly forgive, no failure His grace does not cover, no burden He does not desire to lift, and no person He does not long to embrace. God's grace is His free, unmerited, undeserved favor, which is the essence of His love for us and His desire to have a relationship with us. He already paid the price for our sin by carrying our failures to the cross, and He wants to lavish His grace on everyone who will accept His free gift.

Paul explained this amazing grace: "For all have sinned and fall short of the glory of God, and are justified freely by his grace through the redemption that came by Christ Jesus" (Romans 3:23-24). But surely there is some sin that cannot be forgiven. No, there is always more grace than there is failure, for "where sin increased, grace increased all the more" (Romans 5:20). This is the nature of God and the nature of grace.

Most of us carry in our consciences burdens from which Jesus longs to free us. All we need to do is ask for His grace and forgiveness, and it is done: We are free; our sin is removed; and there is no more guilt, no more shame, no more need for regret. God's grace covers fully, finally, and forever.

Where might you need God's grace and forgiveness in your life? Would you be willing to take time right now to share those burdens you have been carrying for years and simply allow God's grace to wash over you and carry those burdens away? Take time to talk to Him and ask for His forgiveness and grace right now.

RELATIONSHIP, NOT FORMULAS

When we think of how we relate to God, we must go back to the Incarnation. Most world religions have a formula for how humans relate to deity. But there is no formula in a relationship with Christ because God came to meet us on our turf, lavish us with the refreshing rain of His grace, and show us how we could relate to Him through faith.

Jesus had different relationships with different disciples; they were individuals who related to Jesus differently. I do not relate to my two boys in the same way. They are very different individuals, and my relationship with each is based on his personality as it intersects with mine. Likewise I have been married to Mary Ann for thirty-three years, and I have learned that there is no magic formula for marriage. Like all relationships, ours ebbs and flows. Sometimes we grind it out through the stuff of life. Sometimes it feels sweet and intimate. Sometimes we have to work at it, and sometimes it just flows. There is no formula, but our commitment and intentionality keep the relationship healthy.

We should not look at how others relate to God and assume that we will relate in the same way. Each of us is unique, and God will meet us in our uniqueness and humanness as we intentionally seek Him. Perhaps the most helpful chapter in the Gospels for relating to God is John 15, which includes a discussion Jesus had with His disciples just prior to His arrest and crucifixion. He used an illustration He knew His disciples would understand:

> I am the true vine, and my Father is the gardener. He cuts off every branch in me that bears no fruit, while every branch that does bear fruit he prunes so that it will be even more fruitful. You are already clean because of the word I have spoken to you. Remain in me, and I will remain in you. No branch can bear fruit by itself; it must remain in the vine. Neither can you bear fruit unless you remain in me.
>
> I am the vine; you are the branches. If a man remains in me and I in him, he will bear much fruit; apart from me you can do nothing. . . . If you remain in me and my words remain in you, ask whatever you wish, and it will be given you. This is to my Father's glory, that you bear much fruit, showing yourselves to be my disciples. (verses 1-5,7-8)

The key to a relationship with Jesus is found in the word *remain*. Eleven times in John 15, Jesus told the disciples to remain in Him. He taught that if we do not remain in Him, we can do nothing of eternal value because we need to stay connected to His power. But if we remain, we can "ask whatever [we] wish" related to what we need to honor Him, and He will provide it.

Several years ago my doctor told me that I had developed type 2 diabetes. It is a serious condition if not handled well. My pancreas does not produce enough of the insulin my body needs to process carbohydrates. If not regulated, diabetes can lead to numerous complications, including heart disease and kidney failure. But due to modern technology, the doctor also had good news. I could start using an insulin pump the size of a small pager that pumps insulin into my body 24/7. My job is to check my blood sugar once every two hours during the day to regulate the amount of insulin I need and to compensate with insulin via the pump at mealtimes.

As long as I stay connected to the life-giving insulin, my body will stay well. That simple pump is my analogy for the organic connection with Jesus. As long as we stay connected to Jesus by remaining in Him, we will bear fruit and enjoy His presence in our lives. When we do not, our spiritual lives will suffer.

How do we stay connected on a daily basis? Just as I walk through my day always conscious that I am connected to a pump, I walk through my day conscious that I am connected to the God of the universe. That consciousness translates into an ongoing conversation with Him about the events of my day, the challenges I face, the issues I am praying for. The more I practice being conscious of His presence, the more I remain in Him.

How are you doing at remaining in Christ? Are there ways in which you could increase your consciousness of Christ's presence in your daily life?

THE GIFT

Shortly before Christ was to return to the Father, the disciples were understandably full of fear and disappointment. They had finally been introduced to the God of the universe, and now He was leaving them. Jesus made a surprising declaration:

> I tell you the truth, anyone who has faith in me will do what
> I have been doing. He will do even greater things than these,
> because I am going to the Father. And I will do whatever you

ask in my name, so that the Son may bring glory to the Father.
You may ask me for anything in my name, and I will do it. (John
14:12-14)

What an amazing statement! We have the ability to do what Jesus
had been doing? Actually, it fits right in with our premise for this book:
that God created us to be in relationship with Him and to join Him in
His work. We are His agents in this world, bringing glimpses of heaven
to earth.

But how can that happen? Jesus went on to tell the disciples,

If you love me, you will obey what I command. And I will ask
the Father, and he will give you another Counselor to be with
you forever—the Spirit of truth. The world cannot accept him,
because it neither sees him nor knows him. But you know him,
for he lives with you and will be in you. I will not leave you as
orphans; I will come to you. (verses 15-18)

In John 16 Jesus explained what the Holy Spirit will do:

• He will be our counselor, giving us guidance in decisions of life.
• He will convict the world of sin.
• He will guide us into all truth and help us understand God's
  truth.
• He will help us understand the future.
• He will translate God to us as the Spirit of truth resident in us.
• He will empower us to do the work God has given us to do.

While Jesus is the centerpiece of the past and the future, and while
we understand Him in a way we couldn't if He hadn't lived among us,
we are still faced with the dilemma that He is not presently among us
physically. The answer to this dilemma is found in the Holy Spirit, the
third member of the triune God. Paul wrote about the ministry of the
Holy Spirit in our lives:

In the same way, the Spirit helps us in our weakness. We do not know what we ought to pray for, but the Spirit himself intercedes for us with groans that words cannot express. And he who searches our hearts knows the mind of the Spirit, because the Spirit intercedes for the saints in accordance with God's will. (Romans 8:26-27)

When we don't know how to pray, or cannot pray for ourselves, the Spirit intercedes for us with the Father, asking for His help on our behalf. As I lay in the ICU for thirty-two days, either so sick I could not concentrate on praying or in a coma unable to pray, the Spirit of God was interceding for me with the heavenly Father. That is an amazing thought.

The other side of the equation involves us understanding God. How can mere mortals, frail and bound by time, begin to comprehend the Creator of the universe? Again, the answer is by the Holy Spirit. He explains the things of God to us and helps us understand the will of God for our lives. The Spirit helps translate our needs to the Father and the Father's heart to us. That is a gift indeed!

Take a moment and reflect on how the Holy Spirit has helped you in your life and in your walk with God.

ACTIVE LISTENING

Jesus said to His disciples in John 15:14, "You are my friends if you do what I command." No friendship—or any relationship—will thrive unless there is open and ongoing communication. And the most important part of communication, I believe, is not talking but listening. That, too, ought to be at the heart of our relationship and communication with God.

We know that we can approach God with great freedom as our "Daddy" (see Romans 8:15). There are times when we can crawl up onto the lap of God and talk to Him as our heavenly Father. But even more important than talking to Him is listening to what He has to say to us! After all, Jesus called Himself a shepherd of His flock and said that His sheep "listen to his voice" because they "know his voice" (John 10:1-5). God has a voice, and He speaks to us about our lives and our decisions. Thus we need to learn to listen as we pray. That voice can be audible (as Mary Ann experienced when I was in the hospital), or it can come as a deep conviction that a certain course of action is what Jesus wants us to take.

Understanding this concept has changed the way I pray. I now regularly ask God, "Do You have something You want to say to me? I am ready to listen, and I want to hear Your voice if You have something for me." It is an attitude of humble listening and a willingness to be still and allow God to speak to me about issues in my life when He chooses to do so.

The psalms and the great prayers of the Bible are helpful guides for how we ought to pray. We are invited to pray for our daily bread and needs. We are also encouraged to pray that God's name would be honored in our world and that His will would be done on earth as it is in heaven. We should emulate Daniel's prayer of repentance (see Daniel 9), Paul's prayer for spiritual wisdom and insight (see Colossians 1:9-14), and David's prayer of praise and thanksgiving (see Psalm 100).

Too often the focus of our prayers is on our needs, whereas the great prayers of the Bible are often focused on God's will being done on earth and on God's power making a profound difference in our world. To truly understand the heart of God, it can be very helpful to use biblical prayers as our models.

Take a moment to think about your personal prayer practices. Are there areas in which you can grow both in talking and listening to God?

GOD'S LETTERS

A secret to any successful relationship is to never stop seeking to understand, know, and appreciate the one you love. I have spent thirty-seven years studying the love of my life, Mary Ann, whom I met at age fifteen and married at age twenty. With all those years together, I am still learning new things about her. I have also spent twenty-two and twenty-four years getting to know my two boys and their unique personalities.

Likewise, we should never stop trying to get better acquainted and forge a deeper relationship with our heavenly Father. It is absolutely crucial that we study and read the Scriptures regularly if we are to understand the God we serve. Unless we are in the Word consistently, we will find it difficult to remain in Christ, because His Word is truth and life for us. Paul wrote to Timothy,

> But as for you, continue in what you have learned and have become convinced of, because you know those from whom you learned it, and how from infancy you have known the holy Scriptures, which are able to make you wise for salvation through faith in Christ Jesus. All Scripture is God-breathed and is useful for teaching, rebuking, correcting and training in righteousness, so that the man of God may be thoroughly equipped for every good work. (2 Timothy 3:14-17)

Most Christ followers have never read God's Word from beginning to end. If we really want to know and understand God, we need to be thoroughly acquainted with His message to us. Start with the New Testament and read it through, underlining key verses as you go. Then find a good, easy-to-use study tool to guide your reading of the Old Testament. The Bible is not as intimidating as many think. It is the story of ordinary men and women in their relationship with God.

The Scriptures give us God's perspective on issues of life, culture, world events, justice, commerce, and strategic planning. The answers to all of the great needs our planet faces are found in Scripture: how we should treat strangers and the poor, preserve the world God created, relate to people of other races, and confront issues like disease and hunger. Our perspective on our world and its needs will be better informed and influenced by our understanding of God's heart, revealed in His Word.

CONNECTING IN SERVICE

I believe we will be most closely connected to God when we are actively seeking to fulfill His purpose for our lives. Jesus Himself made this point when He spoke of the day when He would come in glory and sit on His heavenly throne. All the nations will be present, along with all people who have ever lived. Then He will separate the sheep (His followers) from the goats (those who did not follow Him). Read carefully what He said to the sheep:

> Then the King will say to those on his right, "Come, you who are blessed by my Father; take your inheritance, the kingdom prepared for you since the creation of the world. For I was hungry and you gave me something to eat, I was thirsty and you gave me something to drink, I was a stranger and you invited me in, I needed clothes and you clothed me, I was sick and you looked after me, I was in prison and you came to visit me."
>
> Then the righteous will answer him, "Lord, when did we see you hungry and feed you, or thirsty and give you something to drink? When did we see you a stranger and invite you in, or needing clothes and clothe you? When did we see you sick or in prison and go to visit you?"
>
> The King will reply, "I tell you the truth, whatever you did for one of the least of these brothers of mine, you did for me." (Matthew 25:34-40)

In other words, our active involvement with people — the hurting, marginalized, needy, sick, and hungry — is work we do for Him. And in doing it for Him, we join Him in His work in our world. When we serve the poor and marginalized, our hearts become sensitized to issues we were not aware of previously. When we care for the hurting, we develop the compassion of Christ. When we share the good news, we become carriers of hope as Christ was. Every time we engage in His work, we connect more closely to His heart and therefore to His purposes for our world.

A LIFE OF WORSHIP AND FELLOWSHIP

Relating to God is really about living a life of conscious connection to Him, fellowship with Him, and worship of Him. He is the only One worthy of our worship, and it is in our worship that we enjoy His presence. Worship is not primarily about singing songs in a church service. It is giving Him our time, service, obedience, emotions, heart, and intellect. It is living for Him above all else and desiring that He be glorified and magnified in our lives.

Nothing about our actions or attitudes should be disconnected from our relationship with God. In every area of life, we are conscious of His presence and our desire to please Him. We worship God in our desire to live in relationship with Him and live out our purpose for Him. I can worship Him as I fish the Gallatin River, and I can worship Him as I carry out my vocational responsibilities. We worship Him as we live wholeheartedly for Him!

Worship is all about saying yes to God in every way we know how. There is no greater adventure than that of walking our life's journey with the God who became like us so that we could become like Him.

THE BOTTOM LINE

We were made for relationship with God, and there is nothing that compares to a living and vital connection with Jesus Christ. We cannot earn it and we do not deserve it—but He offers it to all who will accept His free gift of forgiveness and grace. There is no sin and no person God does not long to forgive and liberate. All we need to do is ask, and He will gladly do it.

Our relationship with Christ is all about remaining in Him, staying close to Him, listening to His voice, and allowing His Spirit to empower us so that we say no to sin and yes to righteousness. There will be times when we feel close and times when we don't, but we know God is always present with us because Christ has given us His Spirit to reside in our human bodies.

REFLECTIVE PRAYER

Father, I want to declare my love for You and my desire to follow and serve You. I thank You for invading this sinful earth with Your hope, truth, forgiveness, and life. I ask You to be the Lord of my life, to give me Your Spirit, and to help me live in connection with You. I am ready to serve You with all that I am and join You in Your work in this world as I look forward to that day when I will live in Your presence forever. Amen.

For Group Discussion

- Share how you relate to God and what practices have been most helpful to you in staying connected with Him.
- Share your experience with the Holy Spirit and His presence in your life. How has He worked in your life?
- Can you think of times when God has clearly spoken to you on some issue? If you are willing, share the circumstances.
- What are your practices regarding Scripture reading? What obstacles keep you from studying God's Word more?
- In what areas has this chapter challenged you to relate to God in a different way?

Chapter 9

WILL I SAY YES TO GOD?

RESPONDING TO THE CREATOR'S CALL IN GOOD TIMES AND BAD

Come to me, all you who are weary and burdened, and I will give you rest. Take my yoke upon you and learn from me, for I am gentle and humble in heart, and you will find rest for your souls. For my yoke is easy and my burden is light.

— MATTHEW 11:28-30

It was one of those wonderful October days when summer collides with fall that Zach woke up looking forward to what lay ahead. Along with members of his junior high group from Two Rivers Church in Knoxville, Tennessee, he was eager for more good, clean fun.

The group finished its breakfast and headed for one of the coolest adventures of the camp: the zip line — where fear meets courage and the experience of a forty-five-mile-an-hour hurtle through space proves that your courage is stronger than your fear. Zach climbed up the ladder, perhaps with butterflies in his stomach. From above, the height is far more dramatic than it appears from below. His helmet was on, and he was attached with the safety gear to the line. With a push, he was off for a thrilling ride.

Instead, it was a ride into tragedy. Onlookers quickly realized the trouble as they watched Zach speed toward the middle of the line. Typically, zip line users would zoom past the midpoint, slow down as the line went upward, and then settle to a stop back at the middle. Counselors would then roll a bulky ladder-and-platform structure into position to take the kids off the line and back down onto solid ground. The ladder was similar to the steps used to roll up to airplanes, except this one, made by the camp and used thousands of times, was constructed of heavy lumber.

But this time the structure had not been wheeled out of the way. There was Zach, oblivious to the danger, his head turned to the side as he raced toward an inevitable collision.

He hit the structure at about forty-five miles an hour, knocking it over and down into a ravine, breaking his helmet, and fracturing his skull like a spiderweb as his friends looked on in horror.

Zach's buddies — the junior high boys and adult volunteers — righted the massive timber ladder and, with superhuman effort, rolled it to where Zach was hanging unconscious and bleeding from the ears.

His parents, Shawn and Sally, were away from their home, enjoying the fall weekend by camping in the mountains. Their getaway, made possible because both Zach and his sister, Kelly, were on the retreat, was interrupted with a call no parent ever wants to receive. They rushed to the hospital, ninety minutes from where they were camping. For three days Zach lingered on life support while the question of survival hung in the air. Many of those who had prayed for me in my illness now uplifted Zach, waiting, wanting, pleading with God for the same miracle that had rescued me.

It was not to be. On the morning of October 8, it was determined that Zach's brain was no longer functioning. How can one describe the feelings after such a loss? Shocking, devastating, overwhelming — these are only the beginning. Shawn and Sally drew some comfort from the knowledge that Zach's last conscious thought and moment was that joyful ride.

Like many who have loved ones in medical emergencies, Shawn and

Sally had put up a blog so that the thousands who were aware and praying could be kept up to date. This is what they wrote on the Caring Bridge website on the afternoon that they said good-bye to their precious son, knowing they would never see him again on this earth:

We are writing this on the way home from the hospital with our amazing friends John and Angel. We are incredibly happy to be heading home, although devastated to be without our beautiful son, Zachary.

We want to thank all of you who came to the hospital to show your support and love for Zach and us. Many of you made huge sacrifices to make the trip over and over. Many of you stayed the night, brought food and gifts, gave us your shoulder to cry on, prayed with us. We also want to thank the thousands of people, a lot of whom we do not know, who have been praying faithfully and fervently since they first heard of Zach's accident. PLEASE DO NOT FEEL LIKE YOUR PRAYERS WERE NOT ANSWERED!!!

We prayed, and listened to others pray, that God would heal Zach. That is obviously what we wanted more than anything in the world, to have our son back, healthy and whole. However, we very quickly came to the conclusion that our prayers were not complete unless we added the very important words, "Thy will be done." We let God know that we would love Him and serve Him even if He decided to take Zach home with Him. We hoped and prayed that God would do a miracle and heal Zach. However, we tried to prepare ourselves for the possibility that God had a different plan for Zach's life.

Zach became a Christian and was baptized by Jon, with his cousin Cody, last year. He was so incredibly excited and we were so proud of him. Over the past year, he really was trying to learn more about what it meant to live the Christian life. He loved going to The Mix (the middle-school youth group at church), going to his small group with seventh-grade boys from the church, reading the Bible with his dad, and praying with us.

We know that he is with Jesus in heaven right now. We know that when he rode the zip line, he was not looking ahead and did not see the obstacle in his way. So we know he never experienced fear or pain. In fact, we truly believe that he rode that zip line all the way to heaven where he landed right in the lap of his Lord and Savior!

We know that those of you who know Zach are hurting and will miss him so much. We know that we will never be able to fill the hole in our hearts that was caused by losing Zach, but we know that eventually the pain will subside. We know we need to go through this painful grieving process, but even so, we will choose to rejoice in our sufferings. In other words, even through the pain and grief, we will choose to thank God for the twelve years He gave us the incredible gift of Zachary.

Shawn, Sally, and Kelly

The question posed in this chapter reaches to the heart of this book—our legacy, our faith, and the call of God on our lives. How will we respond to God? How will we respond when God calls us to an obedience that requires us to change our lifestyles, deal with sin, and conform to His image? How will we respond when we are successful and God gives us wealth and options, when life is good, and when our prayers are answered? And how will we respond in the hard times when sorrow, difficulty, and heartache flood our lives? Will we have the attitude embraced by Shawn, Sally, and Kelly—"Thy will be done"?

Bookstores are filled with books promising that if you just follow simple formulas, your life will fall into place, you will experience good karma, or you will understand the "secret" that attracts unlimited happiness, prosperity, and health. Many of those books declare that this is what Jesus promised and that He will give you the keys to health, wealth, and success. But is this really what Jesus promised?

As I travel the world, I meet men and women who suffer regularly for their faith. Many more—thousands—die every year simply because they are Christ followers. Should I assume that they did not get the memo about a life free from disease, suffering, or persecution? What do we say about the 3.5 billion people around the globe who eke out an existence on three dollars a day or less, with little or no accessibility to health care?

We will experience trouble and hardship as we follow Christ. It is part of living in a broken world, and it is part of following Christ. Not only does He have the power to redeem our suffering for His good, but in the midst of it He is also able to give us something the rest of the world does not know — supernatural peace.

RESPONDING IN SUFFERING

The question is not *whether* we will suffer but *how* we will respond to it when it happens. A proper view of suffering requires a proper view of God and His work in our lives. It requires that we believe God is sovereign over all events of life, even though we do not understand how those events fit into the larger picture of what God is doing. It is believing Paul's words in Romans 8:28: "We know that in all things God works for the good of those who love him, who have been called according to his purpose."

To make clear what the "all things" include, he went on to say, "Who shall separate us from the love of Christ? Shall trouble or hardship or persecution or famine or nakedness or danger or sword?" (verse 35). These are the realities of human existence, Paul said, but none of them can separate us from God.

I have often been asked, "Why do you think God allowed you to get so sick, linger on the edge of death for three weeks, and basically take a year of your life to deal with health problems?" My answer is, "I have no idea." And, "I really don't ask why." God knows why; I do not — and that is sufficient. I do not need to know. What I need to be assured of is that God knows, He has a plan for my journey, and He will redeem it for His purposes. I can trust Him with what I don't understand, knowing that one day it will make sense.

What I do tell people is what I have learned through the experience — about myself, about God's grace, about His love, about what the event has caused me to think about. I could fill a book with lessons that I have learned in the past twelve months.

Every time we are faced with pain, suffering, disappointment, and hurt, the question before us is, "How will I respond to God?" What He desires is a response of faith as we believe in His promises and His faithfulness, even though we cannot answer all of the *why* questions. We know that He will be glorified in and through our lives as we respond in faith.

RESPONDING THROUGH OBEDIENCE

The Christian life is a journey of intentional response to God as He shows us areas of our lives where transformation is needed. The writer of Hebrews put it this way: "Let us throw off everything that hinders and the sin that so easily entangles, and let us run with perseverance the race marked out for us" (12:1).

The writer urges us to get rid of two categories of things in our lives so we can run our race unhindered. The picture here is of races in Roman times when robes would come off and athletes would run with only a loincloth (ancient underwear) or naked so that nothing would get in the way of their running.

The first category of things we're to shed is "everything that hinders." The writer was not referring to sin but was suggesting that just as athletes take off their cumbersome clothes, so we ought to "travel light" and not allow even good distractions to hinder us from living lives of service and ministry. Mary Ann and I have intentionally fostered a simple lifestyle for this reason. By keeping life relatively uncluttered and pared down, we have the time and margin to invest our lives in God's business. Everyone needs to determine what that means for himself or herself, but it is definitely worth exploring.

One of the clues as to whether there are too many distractions in your life is to ask the question, "Do I have the time I need to be involved in service in line with my sweet spot?" If we do not have time for ministry, it means we are not traveling lightly enough. One advantage for those in the developing world is that they must, by necessity, travel light. The *good* things of life available to us can actually distract us from the *great* things—even from our central purpose.

The second category of encumbrance we need to shed is "the sin that so easily entangles." It's a great phrase because sin does just that. It trips us up, keeps us from running the race well, causes us to get distracted, fall, and injure ourselves. There is nothing the evil one wants more than to keep us entangled in our greed, addictions, worries, envy, unforgiveness, self-importance, pride, selfishness, or any number of other sins.

As Christ followers we have a direct responsibility to get rid of the sin that entangles us. In Ephesians 4:22-24 we read these words:

> You were taught, with regard to your former way of life, to put off your old self, which is being corrupted by its deceitful desires; to be made new in the attitude of your minds; and to put on the new self, created to be like God in true righteousness and holiness.

Paul followed these verses with a list of things that need to be put off and things that need to be put on. We are to put off dishonesty, anger that leads to sin, stealing, unwholesome talk, bitterness, rage, brawling, slander, malice, sexual immorality, impurity, greed, obscenity, foolish talk, coarse joking, and debauchery. We are to put on a new attitude of righteousness, holiness, truthfulness, kindness, compassion, forgiveness, love, goodness, thanksgiving, submission to one another, and encouragement to one another (see Ephesians 4:25–5:21).

While Jesus has forgiven our sin and filled us with the Holy Spirit, it is our responsibility to cooperate with the Spirit, to consciously take the steps necessary to get rid of those dark areas of our lives, and to embrace those new character traits of God.

Take another look at the traits we are to put off. Each of those traits contributes to personal dysfunction, addiction, the hurting of others, or the hurting of ourselves. But as we actively pursue the godly traits we are commanded to put on, we experience freedom and the ability to serve and influence others—a life of no regrets.

One is a life of regret, dysfunction, unhappiness, and selfishness; the other is a life of freedom, personal and emotional health, and unselfish service. The question is, which life will we say yes to?

MAKING SPACE FOR GOD

Taking off sin that entangles and distracts is all about making space for God in our lives. Our sin and destructive habits are dangerous for many reasons, but perhaps most of all because they take up precious space in our lives that God wants to fill. The greatest danger in our sin and addictions is that they crowd out the God who made us, the only One who can give us true life satisfaction. As we pursue forbidden pleasure, we give up real satisfaction.

Sin is the evil one's lame substitute for the deep satisfaction God meant us to have. Sin is a fake! A knockoff! I had a conversation once in Chiang Mai, Thailand, about a Polo shirt that was clearly a knockoff. I pointed out to the sales lady that it was a fake because it had a pocket in a place where the real Polo wouldn't have had one. She looked at me in all seriousness and said, "Yes, but it is a genuine fake."

The amazing thing is how often we accept that a genuine fake can substitute for the real thing. The truth is that sin progressively robs us of happiness, joy, and satisfaction because it squeezes out space that God wants to fill. Either we create healthy spaces where God can fill our lives, or we fill them with cheap knockoffs.

Choosing to follow Christ is an ongoing, moment-by-moment process of putting off those things that God reveals to us as wrong, destructive, or simply unhelpful and putting on those things that are good, pure, and Christlike. Every time He reveals to us things we need to put off or put on, we are faced with the choice: Will we say yes or no to God?

Take a moment and think about areas in which you know God is speaking to you but you have not yet said yes to Him.

RESPONDING WITH OUR MINDS

How we think and what we feed into our minds have a profound influence over who we truly are. We are constantly bombarded with information and messages that, from God's point of view, are profoundly wrong. Truth has become a rare commodity in our world.

Many believers say they embrace certain truths, but their lives contradict their stated beliefs. When pollsters look at the behaviors of those who claim to be Christ followers and those who do not, they find very little difference in actual life choices. What this tells us is that even for many Christ followers, truth is relative.

How quickly truth becomes relative when it is inconvenient for us! I call this a "negotiated followership of Christ." It is saying, "I will follow You when it is convenient for me, but I reserve the right to do my own thing when it is not." That is different from a "nonnegotiated followership," which acknowledges that following Jesus is not always convenient, but it is right and true and good; therefore, it is how we choose to live.

This is not just a matter of what we choose to do. It is a matter of how we choose to think because our actions reflect our thoughts, convictions, and beliefs. Paul put it this way:

> Therefore, I urge you, brothers, in view of God's mercy, to offer your bodies as living sacrifices, holy and pleasing to God—this is your spiritual act of worship. Do not conform any longer to the pattern of this world, but be transformed by the renewing of your mind. Then you will be able to test and approve what God's will is—his good, pleasing and perfect will. (Romans 12:1-2)

The key, according to Paul, is what we do with our minds. This means saturating ourselves with God's Word and His truth so that we start to think as He does. God wants to challenge our thinking on many issues that are dear to His heart: justice for the marginalized, help for the hungry and poor, care for the sick, equality for all races, humane immigration policies, provision for widows and orphans, and concern for the environment, to name a few.

Are there areas where you know that you have allowed a convenient relativism to crowd out God's truth in your life?

RESPONDING WITH LOVE

Perhaps nothing defines our response to God more than a life of love toward our friends, neighbors, strangers, and even enemies. Our love for others is a reflection of God's massive love for us. The apostle John wrote,

> This is how we know what love is: Jesus Christ laid down his life for us. And we ought to lay down our lives for our brothers. If anyone has material possessions and sees his brother in need but has no pity on him, how can the love of God be in him? Dear children, let us not love with words or tongue but with actions and in truth. (1 John 3:16-18)

However God has gifted us, He calls all of us to love one another. Whatever else contributes to our legacy, our practical demonstrations of love toward one another will always be central. It is something all of us can do and are called to do. Unconditional love for one another — even for our enemies — is essential to our wholehearted response to God.

How are you doing at loving those around you in practical ways?

RESPONDING WITH TRUST

Our willingness to respond to God fully depends on our ability to trust Him completely. Do we believe He is always good? Are we convinced that His way is truly the best way, even if it doesn't make sense to us in the moment? To the extent that we are willing to trust, we will be willing to respond. Proverbs 3:5-8 highlights this issue as it contrasts trust in God with trust in ourselves:

> Trust in the LORD with all your heart
> and lean not on your own understanding;
> in all your ways acknowledge him,
> and he will make your paths straight.

Do not be wise in your own eyes;
    fear the LORD and shun evil.
This will bring health to your body
    and nourishment to your bones.

To the extent that we choose to acknowledge the Lord in our lives, He will go before us and make our "paths straight." The more we choose to trust and follow, the greater His work will be in our lives. It is the question of whose wisdom is true wisdom — ours or God's?

To make the point even clearer, Solomon told us to "fear the LORD and shun evil," which will bring health to our bodies and nourishment to our bones. The books of wisdom in the Old Testament place a great emphasis on "the fear of the LORD." There is much wrapped up in that phrase. It is about acknowledging God as the sovereign Creator, living with respect for Him and His ways, choosing to say yes to Him in all areas of life, and keeping away from all that is evil.

Life is really a series of choices: We can fear the Lord and follow His way, or we can ignore the Lord and go our own way. Each choice is an opportunity to live either in greater wholeness and blessing or in brokenness and lack of God's blessing. At the core is a life decision we make to trust that God's way is the right, best, and healthy way.

Let's be honest: It is not always easy to bend our will to His. We make choices all the time, and those choices reflect a commitment either to trust Him with all our heart or to rely on our own understanding, to do His thing or to do our own thing. Choosing to trust Him, follow Him, and obey Him is foundational to living like you mean it.

GOD'S PERFECT GOODNESS

When I was in the hospital hovering between life and death, a colleague of Mary Ann's, an art teacher at the high school, gave us a great gift. Knowing how grave my situation was, he stayed up all night and painted the most amazing picture of Christ on the cross. On the back of the canvas, Todd wrote, *Mary Ann, this is a one-of-a-kind picture of Christ. The only one. Todd.* Rarely have I seen a painting that so well captured the love of Christ for us on the cross as this one. It was painted for me.

Mary Ann immediately brought the painting into my ICU room, and it was a powerful message for everyone who saw it. As word got around, nurses from other units came to look at it. Here I was, hooked up to numerous machines trying to keep me alive, in a coma, the ventilator breathing for me, uneventful hours punctuated by times of crisis and emergency—for more than a month. Did God care? All visitors had to do as they came and prayed for me was look at this painting of Jesus (also facing death) on a cross, suffering far more than I ever could. One of my relatives said the hopelessness of my situation was put into context only by the suffering Christ in that painting.

The picture illustrates what Paul wrote in Philippians 3:10-11: "I want to know Christ and the power of his resurrection and the fellowship of sharing in his sufferings, becoming like him in his death, and so, somehow, to attain to the resurrection from the dead." Any suffering we endure is simply sharing in the suffering of the One who suffered so much for us. Paul viewed it as a privilege to do so.

Today, that painting is a centerpiece in our home. Every time I come in the door it reminds me that there is a God I can trust completely, that there is no suffering He has not first endured, and that He was willing to take my brokenness to the cross and die for me.

Where do you struggle with fear and therefore not fully trust in the goodness of God? Consider turning these areas over to a loving God right now.

FAITHFULNESS IN SUCCESS

There is a unique challenge to our response to God when He showers us with material success. Wealth gives us many options, and those options, along with the security we feel from our abundance, present two critical issues: First, will I believe I was responsible for my success rather than God granting it to me? And second, will I allow my heart to wander from wholehearted commitment to God?

When God led the Israelites out of bondage in Egypt to a land He had promised them, He talked to them through Moses about the danger of success:

> When you have eaten and are satisfied, praise the LORD your God for the good land he has given you. Be careful that you do not forget the LORD your God, failing to observe his commands, his laws and his decrees that I am giving you this day. Otherwise, when you eat and are satisfied, when you build fine houses and settle down, and when your herds and flocks grow large and your silver and gold increase and all you have is multiplied, then your heart will become proud and you will forget the LORD your God, who brought you out of Egypt. . . . You may say to yourself, "My power and the strength of my hands have produced this wealth for me." But remember the LORD your God, for it is he who gives you the ability to produce wealth. (Deuteronomy 8:10-14,17-18)

I have met many wealthy people. Some are spiritually disengaged, use their wealth solely for their purposes, and display the hubris that comes from believing they are responsible for their own success. I have also met wealthy Christ followers who display great humility; understand that it is God's wealth, not theirs, and that they are merely stewards; and use their gifts and resources for the advancement of God's kingdom.

Wealth is a gift, but it comes with the danger that we will take our eyes off Christ, His kingdom, and the needs of others. How we respond to God in our success is just as important as how we respond to Him in our need. The greater His blessing, the greater our responsibility.

IT'S ALL ABOUT THE HEART

Response to God is ultimately about what is in our hearts. Do we have hearts that gravitate toward and embrace Christ, or do they embrace our own interests? There are no other options. Either we build our lives on Christ or we build our lives on something else; it cannot be both.

Proverbs 4:23 puts it this way: "Above all else, guard your heart, for it is the wellspring of life." Another translation says, "Keep vigilant watch over your heart; *that's* where life starts" (MSG). It is from our hearts that our actions, words, motives, decisions, passions, priorities, and desires all flow. How closely we guard our hearts affects every area of our lives.

Just as a person chooses to honor and love his or her spouse, we choose whether we will make Christ the center of our lives. Just as I need to make daily decisions that will honor my marriage and my wife, I need to make daily decisions that will honor my Lord and guard my heart.

How do we guard our hearts? We do so by:

- Saying yes to God when we understand His truth
- Taking off those things that displease Him
- Putting on those things that please Him
- Spending time with Him so we can know Him better
- Loving Him through our obedience to Him
- Using our gifts to serve and honor Him
- Committing the whole of our lives to serving Him
- Choosing to trust Him even when times are tough and doubt kicks in

Jesus is the most precious gift any of us could ever have. Saying yes to Him is the most important decision we could ever make. It will affect everything we are, everything we do, and everything we become. Sometimes we do it with a willing heart. Sometimes we do it in obedience, even in the midst of doubts. This is the choice that Shawn and Sally made in the midst of the heartbreaking death of their son, Zach. One month after Zach died, this is what Sally wrote on the family's blog:

Two days ago, November 8, was a day that many people who knew and cared about Zach may have considered a one-month anniversary of his death. This may have obviously brought renewed feelings of pain, loss, frustration, and sorrow. Although we certainly can't and won't tell people how to handle their own grief, we have finally come to the important conclusion that when we focus on the loss, the tragedy, the unfairness, the sadness, and the hurt, we obviously get depressed and end up taking our eyes off Jesus. If we can keep focusing on where Zach is (heaven) and who he is with (God and Jesus), then we are much more motivated to live our lives in a manner that pleases God and makes Zach proud.

I think I said in a previous post that we can simplify the Christian life by concentrating on two commands from Jesus: "And then he told them, 'Go into all the world and preach the Good News to everyone'" (Mark 16:15, NLT). "So now I am giving you a new commandment: Love each other. Just as I have loved you, you should love each other" (John 13:34, NLT).

Many of us are afraid to share our faith with nonbelievers. We don't feel qualified, or maybe we feel that we make too many mistakes in our own lives to tell others about the Christian life. I know I have been reluctant to go out on a limb with many people, especially family members, because I don't want to be rejected or come across as "preachy." My attitude has changed drastically because Zach's life ended so unexpectedly. Losing him has made me eager to share my faith with friends and family who don't believe in Christ. I believe with all my heart that Zach is happy with his new life in heaven. In fact, I am sure that the word *happy* is totally insufficient to describe how he feels right now. I wonder, too, if he might feel some longing and hope for those who have not yet placed their faith in Christ. I am motivated more than ever to show love, demonstrate grace, and live with integrity so others will get a glimpse of the new life we can have in Jesus.

What is your response to God today? Your answer to the question posed in this chapter will affect all aspects of your life — your present, your future, and your eternal legacy.

THE BOTTOM LINE

When all is said and done, it comes down to this: Will I embrace God and His purposes for me completely? Will I respond without reservation? Will I trust His goodness and sovereignty in the life events I experience?

We often fail to understand how deeply God loves us and wants to bless our lives. We don't realize how much He wants us to join Him in His eternal work and how much satisfaction we'll receive when we do. How much of it we experience depends on how closely we follow.

REFLECTIVE PRAYER

Father, I don't want to settle for a relationship with You that is anything but wholehearted. I invite You to be the Lord of all my life in all its parts, and I declare my desire and willingness to follow You with all my heart, soul, and strength. I desire to hold nothing back from the One who held nothing back from me. You are my Lord, You are my Savior, You are my example, and You are my greatest love. Amen.

For Group Discussion

- This chapter described a number of important ways that we need to respond to God. Which of them do you find the most difficult and why?
- What are the spiritual dangers inherent in how we respond both to personal pain and to personal success?
- How can we avoid those dangers so that we stay connected with Christ?
- What do you do to make space for God in your life, and how do you allow God to shape your thinking so that it reflects His values and priorities?

Chapter 10

WHAT SHALL I DO NEXT?

CREATING A PLAN FOR THE YEARS AHEAD

*Who is wise and understanding among you? Let him show it by his
good life, by deeds done in the humility that comes from wisdom.*

— JAMES 3:13

Living like you mean it involves integrating your purpose into everyday
life, carefully deliberating about decisions, and conscientiously managing
your time and energy to maximize your impact for Christ. It consists of
many of the words in the verse quoted above: *wise, understanding, humility, good life.*

The question posed in this chapter may elicit the most practical
responses of all that you've thought through so far, and they may be some
of the most important. That's because we will not become all God intends
us to be until our commitments and intentions are woven into the fabric
of our lives.

I want to show you how a simple tool can help you set priorities, live
with margin, stay focused on God's assignment for you, and develop a
rhythm of life that allows you to be intentional and deliberate. The plan
I use is not complicated, and I can tell you from personal experience (and

from those in our organization) that it works exceedingly well.

It starts with developing a rhythm of life that provides structure on a weekly, monthly, and annual basis. God built rhythm into human existence from the beginning: hours, days, weeks, months, years, years of jubilee, festivals to celebrate key events, and so on. It is almost impossible to live like you mean it without structures that help to frame life.

Many families today have little structure to help them regulate the use of time, energy, talents, and opportunities. The nightly dinnertime together is rare, as are consistent family events or rituals. In our amazingly fast-paced lives sometimes the only common denominators are a last name and the same house in which to sleep. Family life becomes a blur of activity and constant motion—some activities worthwhile, some not. The same is true for us individually. The faster we go, the less intentionality we have—and the less intentionality, the less impact we're likely to have.

In order for us to get a handle on this, we will start at the macro level and work toward the micro level. I will show you what it looks like in real life and give you an opportunity to take a crack at it yourself. This tool will work wonders for you whether you are a high school student, a retiree, a teacher, a CEO, or anything in between. It will help you play to your strengths and get the most out of the rest of your life.

How can I guarantee that this will work? As a leader, I oversee an organization of approximately 550 people scattered across the globe. In thirty years of supervising and leading others, one thing stands out: Those who do not have a plan and are fuzzy about their priorities are rarely effective in their jobs. One of the tasks of a supervisor is to help people stay focused so they will be most productive. When there is limited productivity, one of three things is usually happening: (1) the individual is not working in his or her area of strength; (2) the individual is not motivated, often because of #1; or (3) the individual does not have a plan that spells out priorities and outcomes, along with a rhythm to stay focused on essential activities instead of busywork (time wasters).

If all of that is true in the workplace, it's likely to be true outside of work as well. I am suggesting that we need to be as intentional in every aspect of our lives as we are in the limited confines of our work — not because life is a job, but because we want to make the most of the resources God gave us.

THE ANNUAL PLAN

Let's start with an annual plan. This doesn't mean a list of goals or New Year's resolutions but a plan that identifies our top priorities and a strategy for addressing them. The first thing we do is determine the most vital and significant priorities in our lives and then what outcomes we want to result from them.

By now you have picked up a few basic facts about me: I am fifty-two years old, I have been married thirty-three years, I love to write and lead, and I oversee a global missions organization working in seventy-five countries. As I think of the *Top Priorities* of my life for the coming year, I categorize them as:

- Personal development
- Marriage
- Family
- Work
- Ministry
- Writing

Having identified these top priorities, I then ask what the general outcomes are that I desire for each. I call these *Key Result Areas* (KRAs), and I concentrate on them because they give me specific targets to aim for.

- PERSONAL DEVELOPMENT: Stay healthy in my spiritual, emotional, professional, and physical life.
- MARRIAGE: Keep my marriage vital and growing.
- FAMILY: Stay engaged with Jon as he launches out into the workplace and with Steven as he continues his college education.

- WORK: Provide the highest possible level of leadership and direction to ReachGlobal staff.
- MINISTRY: Use my strengths for the building of God's kingdom in the most strategic ways possible.
- WRITING: Complete a new book manuscript.

Those six KRAs describe the top priorities of my life and the outcomes I want to see at the end of the year. While this exercise seems exceedingly simple, it forces me to identify the six major priorities of my life for the next twelve months. I now have in front of me the specific areas for which I need to develop a plan. (There is no set number of KRAs. Though I've identified six, you may come up with fewer or more.)

The next step is to take each of these desired outcomes and determine what I am going to do to ensure that I accomplish my goals. This differs greatly from typical New Year's resolutions in that I am ***Building a Plan*** for how I will accomplish KRAs. I take at least a day toward the end of a calendar year to determine priorities and KRAs for the next year and to devise the plan I intend to follow.

Why go through the planning exercise? Because once we have a plan, we no longer have to try to figure out what we need to do (that is already done); instead we can concentrate on making the plan happen. Without the plan, execution of the plan is, well, impossible. As you read my example, think of the priorities in your life and what your own plan might look like.

T. J.'S PLAN FOR THE COMING YEAR

My plan becomes more refined as I put specifics under each priority. The following chart shows how this is done.

PERSONAL DEVELOPMENT: Stay healthy in my spiritual, emotional, professional, and physical life.

- Preserve daily unhurried time with Christ, read through Scripture, keep a journal, and communicate with prayer teams monthly.
- Maintain monthly retreat time, annual retreat, prioritize schedule according to KRAs, and delegate issues/tasks that can be handed over to others.
- Read and think regularly on leadership and missions, develop relationships with other missions leaders, and continue to write for the church, leaders, and staff.
- Invite accountability and input from a key group of friends and from my board, and be transparent with staff about schedules and priorities. Keep my prayer team aware of needs and challenges.
- Spend quality time with my "friends for life" on a regular basis.
- Monitor the amount of refreshment that I enjoy so that I don't run out of margin.
- Join Weight Watchers and walk at least one mile per day.

MARRIAGE: Keep my marriage vital and growing.

- Set aside a weekly date with Mary Ann when home, pray regularly together, keep her current with my work, and travel together when possible.
- Encourage Mary Ann in her ministries and affirm her kingdom assignment.
- Find ways to lighten her load and ensure that she gets the refreshment she needs.

FAMILY: Stay engaged with Jon as he launches out into the workplace and with Steven as he continues his college education.

- Take one or two international trips with Steven [he is still in college].
- Be intentional about connecting with the boys in person when in town and on the phone when I am on the road.
- Pray for them regularly and be available to them whenever they need me.
- Try to find at least one extra fun thing that we can do together as a family this year [the kids do not live at home].

WORK: Provide the highest possible level of leadership and direction to ReachGlobal staff. (For the sake of brevity, here I will share the broad plan that has more detail behind it.)

- Provide strategic leadership to ReachGlobal's values, mission, and vision for the future through annual strategic initiatives.
- Build a strong, unified, aligned, strategic, and results-oriented team to lead ReachGlobal.
- Develop current and future leaders of ReachGlobal and influence national partners.
- Mobilize key resources necessary for ReachGlobal to flourish and build for the future.

MINISTRY: Use my strengths for the building of God's kingdom in the most strategic ways possible.

- Use my gifts to help my local church be as strategic as possible in ministry.
- Help other ministries grow in their governance, leadership, and effectiveness. Blog regularly for ministry leaders.
- Teach leadership skills internationally.
- Engage in helping the poor and marginalized in my work globally.
- Encourage pastors who work in difficult circumstances internationally.

WRITING: Complete a new book manuscript.

- Set aside time in the summer for concentrated writing and use travel time for research and writing.

There you have my plan for the year. It is not complicated, but it is specific—and because I have the specifics, I can move to the next level of rhythm. I encourage you to take time when you have finished this book to go through this exercise. You will be better for it. Your life will be more productive because of it. Your impact will be greater with it.

PERSONAL RETREAT TIME

As I described in chapter 4, I set aside time each month for a personal retreat. Sometimes it is a whole day, and other times it is only a few hours. Whatever works for you and your schedule is fine. (Sometimes my retreat occurs on one of those long-haul flights to Asia, Africa, or Europe. However, the time is scheduled into my calendar in advance so it's sure to happen.)

In my personal retreat times, I usually get away to a spot where I will not be interrupted and take along my Bible, annual plan, and schedule. I use this time to:

- Ask the heart question. Always start by asking, "How is my heart toward God?" If we don't get that right, nothing else we are doing will make much difference. Are there areas of my life with which I sense God is not pleased? Am I making enough space in my life for Him? Is there an area of my spiritual life where I need to take the next step?
- Spend time in listening prayer. I try to be quiet long enough that if God wants to remind me or prompt me on some issue, I can hear Him.
- Review my annual plan and ask where I am on target and where I need to make adjustments to stay focused.
- Spend time in God's Word.
- Determine what my top three priorities are for the coming month in order to make progress in my KRAs.
- Review how I did in meeting my three top priorities from the previous month.

- Plan my upcoming schedule to ensure balance between priorities. If I have been considering adding something to my schedule, this is when I think through the ramifications as they relate to priorities.
- Sometimes spend time in a book that will feed my heart.
- Think about life, schedule, current focus, and balance. Where do I need to realign myself in the coming month?
- Review whether I am engaged in ministry as I should be.
- Determine my level of margin and rest, and ask whether I am getting enough refreshment.

If you do this kind of thinking best in the outdoors, do it there. If you do it best on a walk or with some kind of physical activity, do that. Sometimes I do "chainsaw therapy" on my Wisconsin property as I think through these issues. Regardless of the setting, I cannot tell you how valuable this monthly process is to stay focused on the things that matter most. You will be surprised what you figure out or how God prompts you when you ask these kinds of questions.

WEEKLY REVIEW

Our months are made of up weeks, which are another part of our God-designed rhythm. As you think about your previous week, consider just a few "simply profound" questions:

- Did I find space for God in my life this week?
- Was there an opportunity to minister in some way to someone?
- Was I intentional in how I used my time?
- Did I get the necessary refreshment?

A HOLISTIC LIFE

The ten questions presented in this book describe a holistic view of what life is about. God put us here for a reason (*purpose*) and gifted us for that purpose (*wiring*), which allows us to join Him in His work (*legacy*) as we pay attention to the important things (*priorities*) and stay on the cutting edge (*growth*) while living with margin and balance (*refreshment*) as we create ripples with as many people as possible (*influence*), which happens as we remain in Him (*connection*) and say yes to God (*response*) and do all of this with intentionality (*plan*). Each of these questions is connected to the others, so each needs to be asked on a regular basis.

You can realize all ten of those realities in your life. As I said at the beginning of *Live Like You Mean It*, these are the ten key puzzle pieces that will allow you to make sense of the thousands of other puzzle pieces in your life. Getting these areas right will help you get the rest of life right. These questions, and your responses to them, reach to the core of who you are, who God made you to be, the influence your life will have, and the connection you will have with God.

They also are pivotal to the impact that God wants you to have on those around you. We often underestimate what God wants to do through us. His intentions for our impact and legacy are far greater than our own. While our dreams often revolve around wealth, success, or comfort, God's dreams for us involve impact in the lives of others that will transcend time, last for all eternity, and leave an enduring legacy.

Life is never static. It throws us unexpected curves, just as I experienced in the past twelve months. But life can always be right side up if we intentionally orient our inner compass toward God, as we have explored in these chapters. The year 2008 did not go at all as I had planned, but it stayed right side up because of my orientation toward God and my commitment to live intentionally in spite of the circumstances Mary Ann and I faced. My prayer for each one who has thoughtfully read this book is that your life will become that much more oriented toward God—and that, as a result, you will experience His divine blessing on your life.

When I went to the emergency room on December 4, 2007, I never dreamed I would be in the hospital for forty-two days, fighting death each moment. As I have reflected back on that pivotal event, I realize in a new way how quickly our days can end. December 8 was a particularly bad day. I could not breathe and was in terrible pain. I had entered the hospital with only 30 percent of my lung capacity available, and none of the antibiotics had helped because the doctors still did not know what they were treating.

Three things took place that day. I told Mary Ann that I believed I was going to die, they intubated me, and they put me on a ventilator and into a coma that would last eighteen days. The doctors did not believe my body would continue to function if I did not have help breathing. In hindsight, it is indeed sobering to realize that I never should have awakened from that coma. Too many complications took place in those weeks that should have taken my life.

I am deeply grateful that God chose to preserve my life. His goodness would have been no less had He not. But I learned in a new way how fleeting this earthly life can be and the value of making the most of the time He blesses us with. Every day is an installment of grace, to be lived to the very best for His glory.

I ask you a question I have asked myself in the past year: In light of the ten questions, if this were your last day, would you be satisfied with the life you have lived?

That question is not a morbid one but a realistic one. We have no idea how many days or years we have left—every day is truly a gift of grace from God. That is why Paul wrote, "Whatever you do, work at it with all your heart, as working for the Lord, not for men, since you know that you will receive an inheritance from the Lord as a reward" (Colossians 3:23-24).

It is all about intentionality with the time God gives us.

ALL IN?

In these chapters I have shared the stories of many friends. Each of them demonstrates a life of intentionality—they live like they mean it! I wish every member of God's family would discover the incredible joy and deep fulfillment of doing so. If we did, our global impact for God's kingdom would be enormous as each of us made a difference and joined God in our corner of the world. Many of you reading this book belong in the story as well, which is why you have chosen to read it.

Following Jesus is not complicated. It is pretty simple when you boil it down: Love Him and give Him your heart, join Him in His work, stay connected, and be intentional about using your resources. We long for lives of significance, joy, and fulfillment, but sometimes we make it too complex. We look for the secret formula when it is actually found in relationship with Jesus, embracing His call on our lives.

I love the history books of the Bible, the books of wisdom, and the great theology of the prophets and the Epistles. But over and over I go back to the Gospels, where I encounter the living Jesus and am challenged by His clear message of grace, salvation, and love. We could spend a lifetime reading and rereading the Gospels, and we would still be challenged in new ways to follow Him more closely. Get to know Jesus well, be intentional in your commitment to Him, and the life you have always wanted will be yours in abundance.

Jesus gave us an illustration of the response He desires from us in the parables of the hidden treasure and the pearl:

> The kingdom of heaven is like treasure hidden in a field. When a man found it, he hid it again, and then in his joy went and sold all he had and bought that field.
>
> Again, the kingdom of heaven is like a merchant looking for fine pearls. When he found one of great value, he went away and sold everything he had and bought it. (Matthew 13:44-46)

Jesus said that the appropriate response to Him is that we go all in, all the way. This is the only truly appropriate response to His invitation to relationship and to His call. It is an all-in proposition. And so, we conclude with this vital question: "Am I all in?"

REFLECTIVE PRAYER

Lord, I want to be "all in" for You—no holding back. Guide me, through Your Holy Spirit, as I contemplate my personal priorities, my KRAs, and my action plan for the coming months. Help me to use wisely the hours, days, and years You give me and to remain focused on honoring You in everything I do. I give You all the glory. Amen.

For Group Discussion

- Share a section of your plan for intentionality in the coming months or year. Ask for feedback and suggestions.
- What are the barriers you struggle with that prevent you from living as intentionally as you desire? Are there modifications you can make for greater success?
- What rhythm do you use, or think you need to use, in order to stay on track with the important things of your life?
- Have you ever tried or regularly practiced a personal retreat time? If so, what did you find helpful? What were the challenges?

I leave you with my favorite blessing of Scripture and pray that it will be true for you. This is God's heart for you:

> The LORD bless you
> and keep you;
> the LORD make his face shine upon you
> and be gracious to you;
> the LORD turn his face toward you
> and give you peace. (Numbers 6:24-26)

NOTES

CHAPTER 2

1. The online StrengthsFinder can be accessed at www
   .StrengthsFinder.com. StrengthsFinder was developed by The
   Gallup Organization to help people understand their wiring and top
   strengths.
2. You can access this spiritual-formation tool at www.monvee.com.
3. George Herbert Walker Bush, Inaugural Address, January 20, 1989.

CHAPTER 3

1. Randy Pausch, *The Last Lecture* (New York: Hyperion Books, 2008).

CHAPTER 7

1. To learn more about this life-giving ministry, visit www
   .GoDeeperStill.org.
2. If you would like to read one of those stories and learn more about
   GlobalFingerprints, go to www.GlobalFingerprints.org.

ABOUT THE AUTHOR

T. J. ADDINGTON is the international ministry leader of the Evangelical Free Church of America (EFCA), an organizational consultant, speaker, and author. He resides in Minnesota with his wife of thirty-three years and is the father of two children, Jon and Steven (Chip). In his spare time he enjoys reading, traveling, writing, and fly-fishing. He is the author of two previous books, *High Impact Church Boards* and *Leading from the Sandbox: Develop, Empower, and Release High Impact Ministry Teams.* T. J.'s passion is to see God's people be all that they can be.

If this book has helped you or if you have feedback for me, I would love to hear from you at tj@AddingtonConsulting .com. We are all pilgrims on the journey, learning from one another as we pursue our connection with Jesus and our work with Him. Please share with me what you have learned along the way.

Living the Abundant Life!

Learning to Soar
Avery T. Willis Jr. and Matt Willis
978-1-60006-697-9

Just as a mother eagle stirs her nest to encourage her eagles to fly, God "stirs our nest," allowing us to grow in new ways toward spiritual maturity. This book will motivate unfulfilled Christians to respond to God's stirrings and to step out into abundant living.

Discovering the Bible
Gordon L. Addington
978-1-61521-269-9

Take a journey through the Bible in one year. In *Discovering the Bible*, Gordon Addington gives you insightful notes and the historical background for each day's reading. See how God unfolds His amazing plan of redemption throughout the entire Bible. Leader's Guide included on CD.

To order copies, call NavPress at 1-800-366-7788 or
log on to www.navpress.com.

More books from
T. J. Addington . . . Coming Soon!

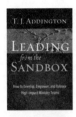

Leading from the Sandbox
T. J. Addington
978-1-60006-675-7

Available April 30, 2010
Learn how to develop, empower, and release high-impact ministry teams within the church to go out into the world.

High-Impact Church Boards
T. J. Addington
978-1-60006-674-0

Available April 30, 2010
Discover how to grow strong, intentional, and authoritative church leaders among a world that is lacking godly leadership.

To order copies, call NavPress at 1-800-366-7788 or
log on to www.navpress.com.